330.126

Financing basic...
cost objection

Exploring the Basic Income Guarantee

Series Editor
Karl Widerquist
Georgetown University
Doha, Qatar

Basic income is one of the most innovative, powerful, straightforward, and controversial proposals for addressing poverty and growing inequalities. A Basic Income Guarantee (BIG) is designed to be an unconditional, government-insured guarantee that all citizens will have enough income to meet their basic needs. The concept of basic, or guaranteed, income is a form of social provision and this series examines the arguments for and against it from an interdisciplinary perspective with special focus on the economic and social factors. By systematically connecting abstract philosophical debates over competing principles of BIG to the empirical analysis of concrete policy proposals, this series contributes to the fields of economics, politics, social policy, and philosophy and establishes a theoretical framework for interdisciplinary research. It will bring together international and national scholars and activists to provide a comparative look at the main efforts to date to pass unconditional BIG legislation across regions of the globe and will identify commonalities and differences across countries drawing lessons for advancing social policies in general and BIG policies in particular.

More information about this series at
http://www.springer.com/series/14981

Richard Pereira
Editor

Financing Basic Income

Addressing the Cost Objection

Editor
Richard Pereira
University of Birmingham
Birmingham, UK

330.126
FIN

Exploring the Basic Income Guarantee
ISBN 978-3-319-54267-6   ISBN 978-3-319-54268-3 (eBook)
DOI 10.1007/978-3-319-54268-3

Library of Congress Control Number: 2017943361

© The Editor(s) (if applicable) and The Author(s) 2017
This work is subject to copyright. All rights are solely and exclusively licensed by the Publisher, whether the whole or part of the material is concerned, specifically the rights of translation, reprinting, reuse of illustrations, recitation, broadcasting, reproduction on microfilms or in any other physical way, and transmission or information storage and retrieval, electronic adaptation, computer software, or by similar or dissimilar methodology now known or hereafter developed.
The use of general descriptive names, registered names, trademarks, service marks, etc. in this publication does not imply, even in the absence of a specific statement, that such names are exempt from the relevant protective laws and regulations and therefore free for general use.
The publisher, the authors and the editors are safe to assume that the advice and information in this book are believed to be true and accurate at the date of publication. Neither the publisher nor the authors or the editors give a warranty, express or implied, with respect to the material contained herein or for any errors or omissions that may have been made. The publisher remains neutral with regard to jurisdictional claims in published maps and institutional affiliations.

Cover image: Détail de la Tour Eiffel © nemesis2207/Fotolia.co.uk

Printed on acid-free paper

This Palgrave Macmillan imprint is published by Springer Nature
The registered company is Springer International Publishing AG
The registered company address is: Gewerbestrasse 11, 6330 Cham, Switzerland

Preface

Work on this book began in late 2014, when the series editor for Palgrave Macmillan's *Exploring the Basic Income Guarantee* invited me to write a book on the question of financing a basic income. The book would fill a significant gap in the literature he suggested and would be an important contribution to scholarship on this issue.

So began the journey of finding authors to help tackle this complex issue. There was substantial enthusiasm for the subject; however, it was viewed as a daunting task by many or their academic and professional lives were just too occupied to take on this subject they deemed very worthy. What is presented within these pages is the effort and analyses of international authors and scholars with experience on the subject of public finance and public program assessment on three different continents. Case studies from North America, Europe and Australasia are included in these chapters with applicable insights for various countries within these regions.

In the two-year period during which this book was being written and edited, we have seen the pursuit of policies of austerity deepen worldwide, while simultaneously the issue of tax evasion and avoidance through offshore tax havens has continually gained more exposure in the popular press. In the United States, the growing gap between rich and poor was a central feature of a very long presidential campaign, particularly before the Democratic Party finalized its choice of candidate for the White House. In some countries sovereign wealth funds (SWFs) have continued to amass wealth for public goods, while other countries have allowed the value of public and natural resources to be squandered. It is clear that there is vast wealth in societies throughout the world, but that it increasingly is consolidated in fewer hands, fewer large multinational corporations and in offshore tax havens that are an affront to the proper functioning of society and management of its public finances. This is the broader international context in which this book has been written. The specific details concern financing basic income, and more precisely a *decent* basic income.

Costly bureaucracies in modern societies do not deliver income security in the way they were originally intended to, and often overlap and contradict each other. Can we not find a way to reorient this wasteful system so that resources are better channelled to ensure universal income security? For a long time the proposed solution has been a basic income, or guaranteed annual income.

November 26, 2016   Richard Pereira

ACKNOWLEDGEMENTS

Cynthia L'Hirondelle and SWAG, Trisha Baptie, Marilyn Waring.
John Kenneth Galbraith, David Suzuki, Tommy Douglas.
Those who worked on and are responsible for the creation of the Croll Report, NAPO.
They and many others leave a legacy and path towards transformative change in the fields of health care, ecological understanding, care work, economics and the foundation of basic income, or guaranteed income.

Contents

1 Introduction: Financing Approaches to Basic Income   1
Richard Pereira

Part 1   Foundations for a Basic Income Guarantee

2 The Cost of Universal Basic Income: Public Savings
and Programme Redundancy Exceed Cost   9
Richard Pereira

Part 2   Cost Feasibility of Basic Income in Europe

3 Financing Basic Income in Switzerland, and an Overview
of the 2016 Referendum Debates   49
Albert Jörimann

Part 3   Building Up BIG

4 Total Economic Rents of Australia as a Source for Basic
Income   77
Gary Flomenhoft

5 Conclusion Richard Pereira	101
Appendix 1	107
Appendix 2	109
Index	113

List of Figures

Fig. 4.1   Economic rent from oil extraction   80
Fig. 4.2   Total Australian land prices 1989–2014   86

LIST OF TABLES

Table 3.1	Gross cost of the basic income in Switzerland (2012)	51
Table 3.2	Earned income/month with BI at CHF 2,500/month and clearing payment scale	54
Table 3.3	Income classes in Switzerland (2010)	55
Table 3.4	Clearing payment	56
Table 3.5	Social insurances, total expenses and part of expenses creditable to the BI account	57
Table 3.6	Hypothetical model for additional income tax for incomes above CHF 30,000 per year	63
Table 4.1	Total resource rents of Australia	84
Table 4.2	Economic rent minus existing revenue	96

CHAPTER 1

Introduction: Financing Approaches to Basic Income

Richard Pereira

Abstract The different ways in which basic income can be financed are set out in this chapter as a guide to reading the book. A decent basic income is presented as the goal of this work, as opposed to some basic income proposals that may be viewed as potentially worse than status quo income security programmes in various countries. Protecting vital public programmes such as universal health care or public education, for example, is essential to implementation of a decent basic income, as is setting it at a sufficient level to ensure a dignified existence and a measure of social inclusion. Proposals that set out to cut public programmes in wholesale fashion and set a low level of basic income are rejected. Income security programme redundancies are discussed in this light along with differing models and methods of financing basic income.

Keywords Basic income · Finance · Financing basic income · Programme redundancy · Demogrant · Public programmes

This book addresses the cost objection to basic income and whether a decent basic income is affordable. What are the public costs – and savings – of implementing basic income? It is important to emphasize

R. Pereira (✉)
University of Birmingham, Birmingham, UK

© The Author(s) 2017
R. Pereira (ed.), *Financing Basic Income*, Exploring the Basic Income Guarantee, DOI 10.1007/978-3-319-54268-3_1

1

that a basic income that is set too low, or below the official poverty line of a society, is not meeting the goal of a basic income as presented in the academic literature and in more common political and popular presentations of the concept. The objective of this public policy is to provide members of a society with the ability to meet basic needs and achieve a measure of social inclusion, even if they cannot find a job in the labour market to provide adequate income to satisfy these basic needs. This book sets out to meet the definitional goals of basic income and it addresses the cost objection by focusing on a *decent* basic income and its financial feasibility.

Also related to providing an adequate basic income is presenting a proposal which does not cut all or most other public programmes in a wholesale fashion, thereby potentially leaving members of a society in a worse financial state than under the current system. Universal public health-care programmes currently in place in many countries, and the provision of free and subsidized public education, are two examples of programmes which if eliminated in order to finance a basic income would create catastrophic costs for many people that could not be covered by the often very modest and low levels of basic income found in most proposals. The prominent work of Charles Murray provides one such approach, which is not supported by this book. Our goal is to provide a much higher level of basic income than found in proposals such as Murray's, while also preserving vital public programmes such as universal health care. We recognize that many public programmes become redundant with the implementation of basic income, and these savings can be directed to financing basic income. What differentiates this book from others is that public programme redundancies are accounted for and treated in a far more selective fashion than in other prominent proposals, and the level of basic income is set much higher than normally found in the academic literature.

Three countries on three different continents are also analysed in proposing a progressive basic income in this study. The combination of ensuring a decent level of basic income and preserving vital public programmes, such as universal health care and others detailed in the following chapters, ensures an analysis of the financial feasibility of basic income which does not undermine or contradict the objectives of this policy initiative. We want to avoid a regressive basic income proposal, which could leave individuals worse off than under the status quo.

Basic Income Models

The two most common approaches to providing a universal basic income are a negative income tax (NIT) and demogrant. The NIT tops up the income of individuals who fall below a certain threshold (this could be the official poverty line, or something higher, for instance). The demogrant refers to a basic income provided to everyone regardless of income. This latter version will usually be paid back in part or in full through existing income tax regimes by individuals whose incomes are above a threshold. The demogrant is paid to all adults and can include provision for a basic income demogrant for children – often set at one-half or one-third of the adult amount for children in many proposals.

A third approach is to pay a universal dividend to members of a society, such as is paid annually in Alaska. This is a type of demogrant, although a variable one which fluctuates significantly from year to year and is usually based on the natural resources of a society. The universal dividend is not a basic income as per the common definition of the term, however if provided at a sufficient level it can meet (and exceed) the goals of a basic income. In this book a universal dividend model is explored as a way to buttress and add to basic income proposals, and possibly provide a superior universal payment as compared with many basic income proposals previously on offer. A universal dividend is based on common wealth in society such as land, natural resources such as oil, forests and minerals, and social resources. A portion of the profits from these common, natural and social assets is shared equally among members of society in a universal fashion.

Combining a basic income with a universal dividend can present a robust new approach to income security in the twenty-first century. A basic income can eliminate (or significantly reduce) some of the most oppressive and inefficient bureaucracies by transferring this public money directly to those most in need, creating a higher degree of empowerment and freedom for those unable to access stable or lucrative employment. It can eliminate a lot of waste of public resources and provide significant public savings. A universal dividend can distribute the excess profits (or economic rent) found in many sectors, particularly where natural resource wealth is concerned, to augment the basic income.

Financing Approaches

Most commonly, basic income proposals rearrange existing income transfers and combine them into a single basic income programme. Welfare payments and their associated bureaucracies are eliminated, and numerous other related programmes are similarly streamlined into one more efficient, de-bureaucratized basic income. Publicly provided pensions, various child benefit programmes the state may have in place, food allowances or food stamps, special tax deductions for low-income households (and tax deductions for high-income households), social housing programmes and payments, charities to address national poverty issues, all can be viewed as partially or fully redundant with a basic income in place. Eliminating much of this complexity and cost can allow for a higher basic income payment than what individuals currently receive from various income support programmes.

In addition to these savings which go towards financing basic income, it is common to discuss a rearranging of the tax system to help finance basic income, particularly a basic income at a decent level. Some proposals exclusively focus on increasing the progressive income tax rate structure already in place, that is, the more income one has the higher the marginal tax rate one pays (see, e.g., Appendix 2 for historical marginal tax rates in the United States). In his chapter Pereira contends that if we first address tax leakages, such as tax evasion and avoidance through tax havens and numerous tax shelters, personal income taxes do not have to be raised to provide a universal basic income. A personal tax cut could be implemented along with introduction of basic income Pereira claims, as savings from programme redundancies are so significant, combined with addressing tax leakage.

Other proposals may focus on increasing corporate income taxation rates, which have been reduced in many countries by substantial amounts in recent decades, as a financing measure. Large-scale government subsidies and tax exemptions for corporate enterprises (corporate welfare) are also often targeted as being better redirected to a universal basic income. Some proposals focus on value-added taxes (VAT) or consumption taxes to raise most or all of the additional revenue that may be needed to finance a basic income. Carbon levies (or a carbon tax) are also promoted to raise and distribute revenues universally, simultaneously addressing environmental policy objectives and income insecurity. James Hansen – former Director of the NASA Goddard Institute for Space Studies – is among the most prominent proponents of the Carbon Fee and Dividend model (often referred to as fee and dividend). Different approaches can be employed or mixed to achieve a desired level of basic income. It is incorrect to assume that personal income taxes must be raised to finance a decent level of basic income. Critics of basic income often assume very large increases in personal income tax rates are required.

Jörimann models a basic income for Switzerland along the lines of a universal demogrant, as opposed to a negative income tax model. While Pereira describes and contrasts both universal demogrant and NIT models of basic income, with no personal income tax increases required, Jörimann does factor in personal income tax rises to achieve the desired level of basic income for Switzerland. The Swiss case study in Chapter 3 proposes a generous basic income of 2,500 Swiss francs per month, or CHF 30,000 annually for adults 18 years of age and above. A lesser amount is provided for children.[1]

Flomenhoft analyses the Australian case in Chapter 4 by focusing on economic rents. What would a universal dividend paid to all members of society, based on economic rent, look like? While Alaska and Norway currently collect large amounts of economic rent primarily from oil resources, and distribute these proceeds for the benefit of society (with only Alaska paying out a universal dividend), they do not capture many other forms of rent that could be used to pay out a much larger dividend. Capturing economic rent from a variety of natural and social resources could result in a universal dividend approximating a basic income, or it could supplement a basic income. The universal dividend based on such rents is also interesting in that it is paid out equally to adults and children – there is not a differentiating amount based on age.

NOTE

1. Charles Murray's plan provides no basic income for children, and for adults it would start at 21 years of age instead of 18, see: *In Our Hands: A Plan to Replace the Welfare State* (2016), and "A Guaranteed Income for Every American" *The Wall Street Journal*, June 3, 2016. This presents a significant problem for the those aged 18–21 who currently undertake large-scale debt loads at this crucial time in their lives when attending university or college, particularly in the United States, Canada or England, for instance where tuition fees are very high and have been rising aggressively in recent decades.

Richard Pereira is Doctoral Researcher at the University of Birmingham, UK, and was formerly an economist with the House of Commons in Canada.

PART 1

Foundations for a Basic Income Guarantee

CHAPTER 2

The Cost of Universal Basic Income: Public Savings and Programme Redundancy Exceed Cost

Richard Pereira

Abstract This chapter addresses the cost objection to basic income, which rests upon the claims that (a) it is too expensive to implement and (b) that personal income taxes will have to be raised to such a high level as to make it politically infeasible. A Canadian case study is used to demonstrate that the cost savings of implementing basic income are often greatly underestimated or neglected, and that personal income taxes do not need to be raised. Personal income taxes could be reduced while implementing a *decent* basic income.

Keywords Universal basic income · Cost · Savings · Public finance · Demogrant · Negative income tax (NIT)

INTRODUCTION

This study demonstrates that a universal basic income (UBI) or guaranteed income at a level sufficient to cover essential needs (at the official poverty line or higher) is affordable. It provides a response to a popular objection by

---

R. Pereira (✉)
University of Birmingham, Birmingham, UK

© The Author(s) 2017
R. Pereira (ed.), *Financing Basic Income*, Exploring the Basic Income Guarantee, DOI 10.1007/978-3-319-54268-3_2

many writers who claim otherwise. Their objection is based on inadequate and/or misleading information. This will be demonstrated by analysis of influential publications in the Canadian context, as well as investigating the basis of the objection in more general, non-geographically specific terms. No cuts to vital public programmes such as health, education, legal aid and so on are sought in this study. Only programme redundancies (sometimes full programmes and partial redundancies in other cases) resulting from implementation of UBI are identified, along with other public revenue losses that can be better directed to UBI. The result is to improve the resiliency of health service delivery and access to education, while ensuring universal income security at reduced public cost.

I will outline the cost objection to UBI in the first Section "The Argument: It Is Too Expensive to give the entire Population Basic Income" and I will then give several responses to this objection in the second Section "Four Responses: Savings and Other Income Sources". In the first response to the cost objection ("First Response: Savings from Replacement of Existing Income Security Programmes"), I will highlight the savings possibilities of a UBI model in contrast to existing welfare models. The second response ("Second Response: Inefficiencies and Leakages in the Existing Tax System – No New Taxes!") will address the claim that personal income taxes have to be raised to an unacceptable level to finance UBI by focusing on tax leakages in the existing system. Bureaucratic costs will then be considered separately as a wasteful element in the current welfare system ("Third Response: Freedom from Bureaucracy"). This will offer additional financing to UBI. The final response ("Fourth Response: Externalities and Current Free-Riding") considers other sources of financing, which could be relied on *if required*. These sources would not require us to raise personal income taxes (or taxes on labour income). This fourth response concentrates on existing economic externalities and free-riding, which if addressed can simultaneously improve the economy, social and health outcomes, and ecological sustainability while raising additional revenue for basic income. An appendix summarizing the findings on programme redundancies and other savings commonly overlooked in the cost objection to UBI is included and can serve as a guide to the reader throughout the chapter.

In proceeding through the study, incomplete calculations of UBI net costs by prominent authors will be evaluated critically. This allows me to conclude that a UBI at a decent level (at the poverty line or slightly higher, distributed to individuals) is feasible, does not require personal income tax increases and can even lead to personal income tax reductions.

The Argument: "It Is Too Expensive to Give the Entire Population Basic Income"

The cost objection to UBI is one of the most persistent arguments against basic income encountered in the literature. It is often reinforced by advocates of UBI in different and unsubstantiated ways. Subsection "A Common Theme in the Literature" will briefly present the scale of this problem and objection more generally. A specific presentation of the objection will follow in subsection "A Country-Specific Illustration of the Cost Objection" based on a case study of one country. This will allow for illustration of major omissions in the objection to begin to surface. Recent Canadian studies that strongly put forth the cost objection will be featured with their most important arguments highlighted.

A Common Theme in the Literature

Critics of UBI, and surprisingly many advocates of the proposal (both strong and weak advocates), claim the financial cost for a UBI at a decent level is out of reach. Critics ignore many savings and other aspects available with UBI implementation. Advocates often fall into the trap of the critics' incomplete arguments by accepting deficient cost assessments as valid. As a result, many UBI advocates claim that although they support the idea and see its many justifications, the cost issue makes it a distant reality or a barrier that necessitates UBI being introduced at such a low level that renders it almost meaningless.

In the case of Van Parijs (1995) – a strong advocate – he makes a novel and useful argument to surmount this artificial barrier, but it is needlessly complex. Readily available, non-controversial and numerous savings and funding sources exist as I shall demonstrate, and Van Parijs fails to properly consider these. He claims UBI will be insufficient unless society reconsiders jobs as collective "assets"; a potentially large new political project that may put off implementation of UBI for an unacceptable amount of time. White (1997) – a moderate/tentative advocate – agrees with Van Parijs that UBI will not be substantial without jobs being considered as collective assets (although White rejects this proposal).

Numerical justification is sorely lacking in these types of prominent cost assertions (Van Parijs 1995: 90, 103–06; White 1997: 315, 321–22, 326). This study rejects the critics' cost objection as well as the weak positions of UBI advocates on the cost issue. Savings arising from implementation of UBI present a much greater amount of financing than both critics and most advocates seem to realize. Van Parijs offers the following perplexing assertion for instance, which is not supported by any evidence, in his prologue to chapter 4, which this chapter and book demonstrates to be unsubstantiated. "Even a very brief look at the relevant figures should tell you that the basic income you have justified in this way is pathetically low" claims Demos, to which the response comes "I know, and this puzzled me for a while.... Moreover, no attempt to spot... more subtle forms of wealth transfer seems to yield anything substantial."

A Country-Specific Illustration of the Cost Objection

In a major study produced for the Canadian Centre for Policy Alternatives (CCPA), a think tank supported by the Canadian Labour Congress, unions and other "national progressive organizations",[1] Margot Young (Associate Professor of Law, University of British Columbia) and James Mulvale (Associate Dean of the Faculty of Social Work, University of Regina) (2009: 24) provide such examples as to the cost of UBI, or Guaranteed Income (GI), for Canada:

Grants paid to Individuals (population data 2006).

Program	Cost (billions)
Grant of $15,000 per year paid to all individuals age 18 and over	$392
Grant of $15,000 per year to individuals age 18 and over, plus a demogrant of $4,000 per year for each child under 18	$418
Payments only to individuals and families below the poverty line to bring them up to the LICO (i.e. reduction of poverty to zero) (2003 data)	$21.5

With the exception of the third option, these are large numbers relative to the scale of the Canadian economy ($1.45 trillion GDP in 2006; over $44,000 for every man, woman and child in the country (Statistics Canada 2007a), and over $1.8 trillion GDP in 2013 (Statistics Canada 2013)[2]). In a separate section of their Table 1, below these intimidating numbers, Young and Mulvale (2009: 24) outline the "Cost of existing income security programs (2005)". These include Old Age Supplement, Child Tax Benefit, Provincial payments to individuals (e.g. income assistance) and four other items totalling $135 billion per year. The net cost of the "relatively generous guaranteed income option" above ($15,000 per adult, $4,000 per child) according to them is $286 billion, and they state that "It thus appears that a full-fledged version of guaranteed income is out of our immediate financial reach" (Young and Mulvale 2009: 25).

In a footnote at the end of the study linked to the $286 billion figure above (n 55), Young and Mulvale write that "This figure does not take account of the additional income tax that would be paid with a guaranteed income system in place. This additional revenue could lower the net cost of the benefit by 20 to 30 per cent" (Young and Mulvale 2009: 34). They do not specify where this additional income tax generation will come from; whether it is from the obvious fact that people's incomes will be higher by the UBI amount, thus corresponding with a higher income tax bracket, or other possibilities in addition to this. And they do not provide the dollar figure of this lower net cost item, which is valued as high as $85.8 billion.[3] Other possibilities for additional income tax generation are numerous with introduction of UBI and Young and Mulvale may therefore be underestimating this aspect. For example, Krozer (2010) explains the economic multiplier effect UBI will have through broadening and deepening endogenous consumption. The removal of labour market work disincentives linked with existing welfare programmes offers greater labour force participation and resulting increases in taxable income, as a second example. Emery et al. (2013: 11–14) provide additional reasons for why productivity and labour-force participation are currently depressed, which UBI/GAI is uniquely suited to address based on their results obtained from analysing other universal income security programmes. Young and Mulvale's total net cost for UBI could thus be reduced by up to $86 billion, and possibly more, on this point alone.[4]

The LICO level Young and Mulvale use above is one measure of the poverty line (low income cut-off), with its after-tax level for a family of 1 person being approximately $15,000 for the comparable years of 2005 and 2006 (but as high as $17,570 in urban areas with populations of 500,000 and over). Families of two persons are deemed by Statistics Canada to have a poverty line income level (after tax) of approximately $18,000 per year under this measurement (but as high as $21,384 in urban areas with the largest populations). Families of three and four persons have poverty line income levels of approximately $22,000 and $27,000, respectively, for 2005–2006 (Statistics Canada 2007b: 18).

In his presentation to the North American Basic Income Guarantee Conference in Toronto in 2012, Jonathan Rhys Kesselman (Professor, School of Public Policy, Simon Fraser University and Canada Research Chair in Public Finance) made similar and stronger claims that a UBI is not feasible in Canada. In a subsequent essay Kesselman (2013) repeatedly claims the cost of implementing a UBI is "gargantuan" and leads off with an example of a benefit of $10,000 per capita. "With Canada's population of 35 million" Kesselman writes, "the gross budgetary cost of this basic income clocks in at a massive $350 billion". He states further:

> Even offsetting this figure by eliminating seniors' cash benefits and provincial welfare, the implied additional cost to taxpayers would be enormous... Income taxes on individuals and businesses as well as other taxes would need to be sharply increased. The general public would not tolerate such tax hikes.... (Kesselman 2013: Section 4)

Kesselman's numbers are repeated by others in the popular press. In a media article reporting on the 2012 Basic Income Congress in Toronto, a $380 billion figure is given as the cost for a universal Guaranteed Annual Income (GAI) in Canada based on Kesselman's presentation (Ternette 2012). The article goes on to summarize Kesselman as stating that the cost "would require a 25 per cent increase in income tax on the highest earners. He said that would not be acceptable to Canadian taxpayers, recommended we forget about a GAI and instead improve our welfare state" (Ternette 2012). Similarly, CCPA Senior Economist and prominent Canadian anti-poverty activist Armine Yalnizyan repeatedly points to Kesselman's work as a deterrent to GAI/basic income, citing the same $380 billion figure as a main reason.[5]

It is important to note how other strong claims are linked to the cost objection, that is, UBI is too expensive, *and the increased taxation required is not politically feasible*. Raising "all households above the poverty line carries severe hurdles of... public finance and political feasibility that proponents typically neglect" (Kesselman 2013: Introduction). Kesselman (2013: Section 4) writes that "the personal tax system would be applied to finance the system". This is a common argument among objectors to UBI based on cost; that the amount of new *personal* income tax that would have to be applied makes it a prohibitive policy.

Four Responses: Savings and Other Income Sources

This section will explore items that the cost objection to UBI fails to consider or develop in reducing the net cost of UBI implementation. Four categories of items will be explored, providing four responses to the objection. The first category and response "First Response: Savings from Replacement of Existing Income Security Programmes" will respond to the savings issue by considering additional available savings from the replacement of existing income security programmes missed by the cost objection. These programmes are often inefficient, wasteful or disproportionately benefit the highest income recipients in contradiction of the original intent of such programmes to provide income security to all. They can be considered to be redundant with introduction of UBI; redirecting these programme funds to UBI can be considered a much fairer universal benefit that comes much closer to the original intent of these various programmes to increase income security.

Subsection "Second Response: Inefficiencies and Leakages in the Existing Tax System – No New Taxes!" responds to the claim that personal income tax would have to be raised to an unacceptable level to fund UBI. This is not true as there are significant leakages in the existing tax system, which can provide a large amount of funding without raising taxes. The next subsection "Third Response: Freedom from Bureaucracy" will consider the cost of bureaucracy. This response demonstrates that bureaucratic costs associated with existing programme spending have not been factored into the net costing for UBI. The final category and response "Fourth Response: Externalities and Current Free-Riding" will consider new sources of income through pricing of current externalities and free-riding as an additional source of financing for UBI (if required). This includes prevention of environmental and social dumping, and curbing harmful activities such as excessive financial speculation.

First Response: **Savings from Replacement of Existing Income Security Programmes**

In this subsection, two leading cost objections to UBI in Canada will be briefly critiqued for their narrow savings considerations. The programme redundancies available by implementing UBI are greater than presented in these studies. A parallel will be drawn with other nations that have similarly elaborate bureaucratic welfare states as Canada. These states should also consider a far greater number of savings items when drawing up cost assessments for UBI at the national level. I will then explain various programmes and existing costs that can be considered as savings if a UBI is implemented – both in Canada and in countries with equivalent programmes and costs. Starting with the Registered Retirement Savings Plan (RRSP) tax shelter, I will demonstrate the redundancies that are missed by the cost objectors in arriving at the mistaken conclusion that UBI is financially out of reach for governments. This is a conclusion only reached by neglecting numerous existing costs that are redundant with, and better addressed by, UBI.

While Young and Mulvale (2009) do identify some of the savings to be realized from a basic income programme, Kesselman (2013) emphasizes the $350 billion cost figure without identifying any total programme costs that become redundant or unnecessary with introduction of basic income. The replacement of some existing income security systems made possible by UBI will provide a significant amount of savings for funding UBI. Young and Mulvale identify seven programmes that are, or could be seen as, redundant with a basic income in place, but do not go further. There are many more programmes and savings to be considered. The seven programmes they list are: Old Age Supplement ($29 bn), Child Tax Benefit ($9 bn), Provincial payments to individuals/welfare payments ($32 bn), GST and other tax credits ($15 bn), Employment Insurance (EI) ($14 bn), Local payments to individuals ($3 bn), and a seventh item treated in a confusing manner because it is first included then excluded in a subset of their Table 1 (with the subset including two other items equivalent in cost), namely Canada Pension Plan/Quebec Pension Plan (CPP/QPP) ($32 bn). The CPP/QPP is properly excluded ultimately by Young and Mulvale because it is a contributory scheme, and I would argue the same for EI which is curiously treated differently by Young and Mulvale and included in the list of programmes to be eliminated with introduction of UBI.

In Canada, as in many other countries, seven such items (or six if EI is maintained) that reduce the net cost of UBI would be considered a very short list. There are many more forms of income security and related programmes that can be considered as redundancies with introduction of UBI, specifically a UBI at the level Young and Mulvale identify which meets the goal of ensuring no individual's income is below the poverty line.[6]

The RRSP programme is one of dozens such programmes that is not mentioned by any of the authors above. It is a retirement income supplement programme and tax shelter that disproportionately benefits high-income earners, contributing to the regressive tax system currently in place (nominally progressive, but regressive once such skewed programmes, benefits, deductions and other advantages are factored in).[7] There was $775 billion of assets in Canadian RRSPs in 2011 (CBC 2013) accumulating tax-free growth from stock markets and other investments. Annual tax deductions alone from the RRSP program (and similar registered pension plan (RPP)) cost the federal government $20 billion per year with two-thirds of this benefit going to the richest 10% of Canadians (Department of Finance 2014: 18; Lee and Ivanova 2013: 23–26; CAW n.d.). This is exclusive of foregone tax revenue on unearned income within this tax shelter. These figures also do not include the provincial portion of income tax deducted and refunded to RRSP (and RPP) contributors. Only 24% of eligible tax filers contributed to the programme in 2011 (down from 26% in 2010) (CBC 2013), as many are too indebted, underemployed, precariously employed, unemployed or working full time and earning too little to have the necessary disposable income to take advantage of such schemes. "Many low-income Canadians can actually be worse-off if they contribute to an RRSP" (CAW n.d.).

Other similar programmes that are not considered by the cost objectors as unnecessary with the income security provided by basic income include the Tax-Free Savings Accounts (TFSAs 2014) tax shelter,[8] Registered Education Savings Plans (RESPs) and numerous other tax shelters with even far less potential to help anyone in need than these three mentioned above (Taylor 2007).[9] Charitable programmes and the associated donation and tax deduction system, with highly favourable tax deduction rates could also be vastly reduced or eliminated with a basic income in place. Whereas almost 30% of Canadians claimed charitable donations in the early 1990s, the figure was 23% in 2011. "Fewer and fewer people are donating larger amounts...And spouses with higher incomes can also claim contributions made by their partners" (Simms 2013). Almost six million Canadian tax filers claimed charitable contributions in 2011. In addition to billions of dollars in donations annually to the "poverty industry" as some have called the growing charitable sector, and the favourable tax deductions associated with them, charities also often receive additional funds and grants from various levels of government, and in too many cases scandalously high salaries and perks are given to executives and managers of these often otherwise well-meaning endeavours – directing these various costs towards funding a UBI could prove far more efficient and be yet another savings element neglected by the studies.

Summarizing up to this point some of the more obvious additional savings not included in the cost objections, one finds up to $86 billion or more in the Young and Mulvale study which they have indirectly alluded to but not calculated, nor have they used this item (additional income tax generation with a guaranteed income in place) to reduce the net cost of UBI implementation as they indicate should be done. Perhaps it is an overly cautious move. If so, their conclusion based on an unjustifiably higher number that "a full-fledged version of guaranteed income is out of our immediate financial reach" needs to be preempted. Perhaps it was an oversight of the study, despite the general point being made in a footnote. This item, and its many dimensions, is likely worth more than $86 billion as I have detailed in Section 1, thus reducing Young and Mulvale's "full-fledged" UBI cost from $286 billion down to under $200 billion. The RRSP programme – and RPP – offers $20 billion in federal tax deduction savings alone (not including supplemental provincial tax rates and associated deductions, and not including tax-sheltered growth or dividend income from corporate shares on $775 billion in RRSP-held assets). This brings the cost of a *decent* UBI down to well under $180 billion. These two items reduce Young and Mulvale's costing of UBI by well over $100 billion, and bring down Kesselman's costing far more.

Eliminating the RRSP programme will also remove the tax-sheltering component of this programme containing assets of $775 billion (as of 2011). Growth of 6% on these assets represents $46.5 billion. For comparison, the Toronto stock market gained almost 10% in 2013 while American stock markets gained between 26.5 and 38% in the same year (Morrison 2013). Lee and Ivanova (2013: 24) show that 0.89% of all tax filers in 2010 claimed 50% of all capital gains (those with incomes over $250,000 per year). If capital gains were not tax sheltered in RRSPs, the highest income brackets that claim a disproportionate majority of this benefit would pay over 40% (CRA 2014a) in tax (combined federal and provincial rates) on this *unearned income*.[10] Applying a more conservative 35% tax rate to $46.5 billion for the sake of estimation produces an additional $16.3 billion in annual savings better directed to UBI (not including dividend income received in RRSPs). This brings Young and Mulvale's $286 billion cost now to below $164 billion; an additional $122.3 billion in savings from two easily identifiable[11] and non-controversial sources ($86bn in additional income tax generation at prevailing rates plus $36.3bn in RRSP programme savings). Their costing, upon which they base their negative conclusion, is 43% lower at this early stage of analysing the proposal.

Tax-Free Savings Accounts introduced in 2008, and mentioned briefly above, represent another inefficient new savings and income security programme. Milligan (2012: 3) writes that "the bulk of the total contributions come from high-wealth families who still make large TFSA contributions on top of any 'float' held outside the TFSA". This programme is similar to the Individual Savings Account programme in the UK, introduced in that country in 1997 (Milligan 2012: 7). Adding new programmes and financial and accounting complexity in this manner (Department of Finance 2009), to benefit the highest income earners makes no sense if the goal is to improve economic or income security for all. Specialized tax advice to co-ordinate these various programmes and numerous details within them for maximum benefit is also only available at significant cost to high-wealth individuals (Milligan 2012: 7; Department of Finance 2009). Using a conservative estimation from Milligan's study of TFSAs I will include a $3 billion annual savings from cancellation of this programme/tax shelter that could be better used towards implementation of UBI. Numerous other non-RRSP and non-TFSA tax-shelter programmes referenced earlier in this section, which are not practical to individually cost here, will be estimated at an additional conservative $3 billion combined.[12] This represents an additional $6 billion of savings not factored into the net cost figures, or $128.3 billion in missed savings thus far.

Several programmes and other public costs are implicated in the annual cost of poverty to society. The savings available in this respect from providing a decent UBI at, or slightly above, the poverty-line income level totals $72–86 billion annually in Canada (Rainer 2012; Canada Without Poverty n.d.; Laurie 2008; Rainer and Ernst 2014). "Poverty's demand on health care alone may now approach $40 billion per year" in Canada (Rainer and Ernst 2014). Reduced public costs for health, crime and other factors make up this large total savings item. If one-third of this cost is stripped out due to some overlapping items with those already presented above, we have $53 billion in average savings per year (2007 dollars), bringing the UBI net cost in Young and Mulvale's study down from $286 billion to $105 billion ($181 billion in missed savings). This is 63% lower than the net cost for UBI presented by Young and Mulvale for their generous version of basic income, and 70% lower than the $350 billion cost presented by Kesselman.[13]

Responding to a leading national newspaper columnist's article critiquing the $32 billion cost of raising all Canadians out of poverty with cash transfers, Rainer and Ernst (2014) reply that the cost of poverty alone is between $72 billion and $86 billion annually. This leads them to ask the opposite question the cost objectors ask, namely "how can we not afford a basic annual income"? The $32 billion "cost" figure, which disappears into a surplus of savings with introduction of basic income, is based on the negative income tax (NIT) version of basic income. We will treat this issue of two versions of UBI (NIT as a "top-up" version of UBI versus upfront payment to all citizens [demogrant version]) at the end of the study, but for now it is useful to continue directly addressing the large figures put forth by cost objection claims as found in Young and Mulvale, and Kesselman. A couple of quotes on this difference are worth introducing at this point though. Young and Mulvale (2009: 15) state that one major Canadian government report in the 1980s "recommended a universal demogrant-based delivery system, rather than a strictly tax-based system [NIT], although [it] argued that either would be effective". Also, Young and Mulvale (2009: 21) indicate that all of their models "assume that a guaranteed income program could be delivered either through a universal demogrant or through a negative income tax".

To conclude this section on savings from programme replacement/ redundancy and reduction directly linked to implementation of UBI I will limit myself to addressing three more programmes and forms of savings. Day-care costs, in its publicly subsidized form and in its extremely expensive private form, can be greatly reduced with a UBI in place. The same will be demonstrated for social housing in various forms. And thirdly, since UBI cost objections are often coupled with advocacy of improvements to the status quo patchwork of welfare programmes, it is not accurate to simply calculate the cost of existing welfare payments to individuals in reducing the net cost of UBI. One must reduce the net cost of UBI by not only existing welfare costs, but also by what the cost objectors are proposing in terms of increased funds towards welfare – this is additional funding they would put towards the (admittedly failed) existing system, which would be better directed to UBI.

Subsidized institutional day care, which advocates internationally recommend should be funded at the rate of 1% of GDP (Canadian Labour Congress 2013), totals over $18 billion per year in the Canadian context. Constantly increasing labour market pressures, arbitrary bureaucratic rules (e.g. excluding people from maternity and paternity leave benefits) and a perverse approach to economic development sees new forms of extended day care being offered. In Canada 24-hour a day day care (an oxymoron), 7 days a week, was introduced in Quebec, with one of the main reasons cited being the accommodation of night-shift casino workers in Montreal (Peritz and Gagnon 2000; CBC 2000). "One pilot project at the Montreal Casino operates 24 hours daily, 365 days a year" and the Family Minister in the Quebec government, Nicole Léger, affirms she thinks it "a good idea" (Dougherty and Jelowicki 2000).[14] It is deeply discriminatory that some parents get extended maternity and paternity benefits (public and private benefits in some cases) to care for a new child, while others feel forced to put their children as young as 6 weeks of age, or even earlier (Québec 2014), in institutions.

A UBI can allow for provision of a decent level of care for all children by parents or those they trust most (family members, close neighbours) when the need may arise. While public expenditure on childcare in Canada is less than 1% of GDP currently, the OECD (2013: 1, 3) indicates that many statistics relating to day care expenses are underestimated because of the reporting methods, or lack of reporting, by various levels of government on these expenditures to national governments (Canada is specifically identified as having this underreporting/underestimation problem). If the advocated 1% solution (costing over $18 billion per year and supported by many UBI cost objectors) is reduced by about half, because of UBI implementation and the far greater number of options it would introduce to provide both parental and non-parental childcare outside of publicly subsidized institutions, we could add another $9 billion in savings or funding better directed to UBI. We could also help stem the tide of increasingly destructive new forms of employment that are creating the growing artificial need for unconventional day care and night care. Among those who claim to need childcare overnight because of a lack of care alternatives, income insecurity or job inflexibility, only one in 10 say they are prepared to leave their children in centres overnight (Peritz and Gagnon 2000). Clearly it is a trend[15] the overwhelming majority want to avoid. UBI can provide better options.

Some other aggressive trends that limit care options for children include: the rise in numbers of multiple job workers[16]; the rise in unpaid overtime work (Pereira 2009); dismissals of pregnant women by increasingly brazen employers resulting in loss of maternity leave benefits (Pigg 2009)[17] and workplace cultures that discourage and penalize employees who take vacation time to which they are entitled (Wadsworth 2013;

Herman 2011; Pereira 2009), despite paid vacation entitlement being inferior in Canada and the US to most OECD nations. This is not an exhaustive list, as the weakening of labour unions and other developments in the past two decades have created intense time poverty in North America, which a UBI can help rebalance to significant degree. $9 billion in additional programme savings annually from childcare (not to mention private child care costs which are extremely high) added to $181 billion in missed programme savings tallied earlier, totals $190 billion and brings the net cost of UBI down to $96 billion (from the original $286bn (net cost), $350bn or $380bn depending on which cost objection argument referred to).

If people had sufficient and secure minimum income that they could rely on through difficult circumstances (without complicated bureaucratic entanglements, stigma or exclusions) they also would not need to resort to social housing and affiliated programmes in most cases. These programmes also limit freedom in terms of where one can live, as most social housing is in selected locations with a limited variety of home types, and most importantly, long waiting lists in many instances. Many Canadians do not have any special needs when it comes to housing, but are in social housing simply because of a lack of sufficient and stable income (Swanton 2009: 20) in an increasingly precarious work environment. And if they have special needs those should certainly be accommodated and provided for while supporting the desire of many with milder special needs for independent living with a decent UBI (and not reducing any of the supporting services they currently receive, a basic principle of the Croll Commission in advocating for guaranteed annual income).

The Toronto Community Housing Corporation is one of North America's largest landlords, housing about 164,000 tenants, with an additional waiting list of over 72,000 (Monserbaaten 2013; Maloney 2014). Canada's 600,000 social housing units receive $3.5 billion annually, cost shared between federal and provincial governments (Federation of Canadian Municipalities 2013[18]). Under the Direct Rent Supplement Programme tenants in Alberta receive money directly from CRCH (Capital Region Housing Corporation 2011: 1) to assist with their housing costs, up to a maximum of $500 per month. Rental subsidies in British Columbia can be up to $683 per month ($8,196 per year) (BC Housing 2010). Different programmes involving forgivable loans that Canada Mortgage and Housing Corporation (CMHC) lists as available to real estate developers are valued up to $150,000 per unit (CMHC 2014).[19]

Global figures for all this housing complexity, including subsidization programmes at the local level of government, are difficult or impossible to encounter. Assuming $5 billion in annual costs and that the majority of people housed in this way or receiving rent supplements are simply lacking stable, sufficient income, UBI could potentially reduce this cost by $4 billion.

The final programme savings item I will deal with (and there are many more) here as indicated is the discrepancy between current welfare expenditures and improvements to the welfare system that UBI cost objectors advocate. While Young and Mulvale point out the $32 billion in annual provincial income assistance/welfare payments to individuals that become redundant with UBI and include this as savings against the net cost of UBI implementation, they also call for easier access to welfare and increased payments for those in it (Young and Mulvale 2009: 31) in lieu of UBI, as is common with many of the cost objections.[20] They do so because they know the existing system is a failure.[21] But they are not willing to commit to UBI. Therefore, the additional funding advocated for the existing welfare system should be added to actual existing welfare payments, as this would be the total amount of spending (savings for UBI advocates) that would be directed to the current system, but available to UBI financing instead. The UBI cost objection studies are not clear on how much they would increase provincial income assistance/welfare payments by resisting UBI implementation. But if we assume a 50% increase is reasonable (and possibly very conservative given both easier access to the system and increased payments for recipients is advocated), then that would add $16 billion in payments. These are pure savings for the UBI advocate, and thus reduce the net cost of UBI to $76 billion (factoring in this $16 billion annual savings with the above $4 billion in annual social housing costs not deducted from net cost yet).

Conclusion: Programme Savings and Redundancy are Vastly Underestimated

The programme savings in this section add up to $210 billion annually. The savings have been conservatively calculated in many respects and could therefore be significantly greater. And there are numerous other programmes that could be included to lower UBI net cost from *programme savings alone*. Universal public health care has not been affected.

There is no intention to cut funding from, or reduce the quality of, publicly delivered health care. Instead, the public health care burden is reduced generating a significant savings in the system with introduction of UBI at a decent level. A major goal of this thesis is to improve health outcomes and to resist any attempts towards privatization or downloading of health costs onto citizens.

This *additional* net cost reduction of $210 billion annually (and proportional equivalents from similar programme redundancies in many other countries) has been missed by the UBI cost objection studies, and thus influences negative conclusions on UBI implementation. Net cost has been reduced by almost 75% of Young and Mulvale's $286 billion net cost annual figure. Programme savings/redundancies reduce Kesselman's $350 billion annual cost figure by $342 billion ($132 billion in savings identified by Young and Mulvale, plus $210 billion in additional savings identified in this work), or 98%.

A few other significant programmes (not a full list) that could be seen as redundant with UBI in place and thereby provide additional savings to finance it include: the Working Income Tax Benefit (WITB), or equivalent EITC in the US which Kesselman (2013: Section 7) calls for increased cash support to individuals through; various "special public employment projects" which Kesselman (2013: Section 7) also calls for increased funding for; and boutique tax benefit programmes such as the Senior Homeowners' Property Tax Grant.[22] I invite others to add to the list savings items that they would see as redundant with introduction of a sufficient UBI to ensure coverage of basic needs, and to cost these items. This study has gone much further in this direction than previous available studies encountered, and has space and resource constraints.

The NIT versus demogrant distinction between UBI proposals (two methods of delivery) introduced earlier in this section should also be briefly noted as a reminder when considering the vast cost differential between the two versions. Keeping this distinction in mind as this study proceeds will allow one to see amplified savings that are more visible with NIT, but masked in the UBI cost objections' general approach and focus on the demogrant model. Recall that two key sources – Young and Mulvale's study, and a major Canadian government report on UBI (McDonald Commission report) from the 1980s – clearly state that both delivery methods are effective with the latter source recommending the universal demogrant version. The importance of this distinction is that the starting cost point identified for NIT is $21.5 billion (Young and Mulvale 2009: 24), whereas the starting cost for the demogrant is $418 billion (Young and Mulvale 2009: 24). Both systems can be "calibrated" to achieve the same results (Young and Mulvale 2009: 21).

Taking the $132 billion in savings from existing income security programmes identified by Young and Mulvale (2009: 25) to reduce UBI cost from $418 billion to a net cost of $286 billion, plus the additional savings identified in this section valued at $210 billion, totals $342 billion in savings. Applying this against the insignificant NIT cost for UBI, results in a large-scale surplus of over $300 billion. The demogrant version cost is not as far off the NIT cost as implied.[23]

Second Response: Inefficiencies and Leakages in the Existing Tax System – No New Taxes!

This response will be brief in identifying major areas of tax revenue losses at prevailing rates that could help finance a decent UBI. No new taxation is involved in the analysis. The evasion and avoidance of taxes by those best positioned to take advantage of tax complexity and lax enforcement in specific areas is the concern, and UBI cost objections do not give this sufficient attention. Instead, cost objectors by default resort to the "need" to tax personal/labour incomes at higher rates in order to deal with the unacceptable high cost of UBI and the financing gap it purportedly generates.

The exclusive reliance on the personal income tax system as the only vehicle for addressing the costs of UBI by cost objectors such as Kesselman, Young and Mulvale – although in other places Kesselman, for example, mentions business taxes as well before reverting to this more exclusive argument and emphasis on the personal system – is misplaced, in several ways. Van Parijs, White and many other international writers on UBI also emphasize the need to tax labour much more aggressively in order to successfully finance basic income, although supportive of the basic income idea. "The personal income tax system would be applied to finance the [basic income] system" Kesselman (2013: Section 4) writes in a section entitled "Basic income: Gargantuan costs, unacceptable tax hikes". Young and Mulvale also state that:

> Any version of guaranteed income – whether universal or targeted,... demogrant or through a negative income tax [NIT] – obviously involves

substantial government spending. Raising taxes is politically unpopular. So committing substantial public revenue to ensure basic economic security for all is seen by many as beyond the realm of the "reasonably discussable". (Young and Mulvale 2009: 23)

This study has thus far disproved the above strong claim that negative income tax "obviously involves substantial government spending" because in fact there are large-scale savings to be gained (a surplus) by introducing UBI in the NIT form (and in the demogrant form as will be made clearer later). It has already been established (Subsection "First Response: Savings from Replacement of Existing Income Security Programmes") that NIT and demogrant versions can achieve the same results through calibration and that both can be equally effective, with one major government report favouring demogrant delivery over NIT in assessing both versions for optimal cost and effectiveness. Therefore, if Young and Mulvale (2009: 24) produce a $21.5 billion cost figure for a negative income tax version of UBI that achieves "reduction of poverty to zero", and they produce a limited savings list of redundant programmes valued at $132 billion as a result of UBI implementation, there is no need to talk of massive spending involved. What we have is large-scale savings – even if we remove several items from Young and Mulvale's list of savings.[24]

It is confounding when this information is presented and conclusions are reached that a decent UBI appears to be "out of our immediate financial reach" (Young and Mulvale 2009: 25). If taxation is to be discussed, it must start with the existing system and where it is failing to collect legal revenues at prevailing rates. Canada Revenue Agency (CRA) states "When an individual or business does not fully comply with tax legislation, an unfair burden is placed on law-abiding taxpayers... and the integrity of Canada's tax system is jeopardized" (CRA 2014b). The most significant item in this regard is offshore tax havens and the tax evasion and avoidance that occurs through them.

Vast wealth is channelled away from public goods through these shady and secretive offshore jurisdictions, placing additional burdens on those in lower income brackets. Addressing this as a priority, before referring to any personal income tax increases, is a necessity as the existing system is not being honoured or enforced. Related issues of transfer pricing used as a mechanism to artificially lower profit figures, and therefore taxable income, by major corporations also needs to be addressed on the tax side before objecting to programme costs, even if the costs for UBI are overestimated. Such issues deal directly with the existing tax system as it stands, and the priority is to ensure fair and progressive rates of taxation are actually collected under current rules before raising the scare of personal income tax increases. During this "golden age for corporate profits" some of the largest multinational companies are paying zero tax, and receiving tax refunds and subsidies simultaneously (Buchheit 2013).

> How many Canadian tax dollars are we losing to tax havens?... There are three independent estimates that put the figure as high as $80 billion a year that federal and provincial governments are losing to various forms of tax evasion. A recent Statistics Canada report showed that a quarter of all Canadian direct investment abroad was going to countries that have been identified as tax havens. Barbados was the destination for $53 billion in 2011. (CPJ – Citizens for Public Justice 2012; Canadians for Tax Fairness n.d.)

As concerns developing countries, tax havens facilitate transfer pricing, capital flight and corruption worth 10 times the value of aid received by these countries (CPJ 2012). In the UK one of numerous high-profile stories recently involved the American multinational company Starbucks repeatedly claiming annual financial losses despite making billions of pounds in profits. Transfer pricing allows such corporations to use offshore tax havens and other mechanisms to misprice transactions between companies in a group (Clinch 2012). The issue affects all countries and their ability to provide public goods, including UBI.

If we take the $342 billion in total savings available from UBI implementation identified thus far ($132 billion in savings from Young and Mulvale's net costing plus additional savings of $210 billion detailed in Subsection "First Response: Savings from Replacement of Existing Income Security Programmes") and add the $80 billion in tax leakage from Canada to offshore tax havens each year, a large surplus is further built up by implementing the NIT version of UBI, as well as surpluses achieved by implementing the demogrant version of UBI as costed by multiple proposals in the cost objection. And recall there is little difference between both NIT and demogrant versions in the final analysis, which has not been clarified sufficiently in the cost objection.

To be conservative let us take half of the amount of the $80 billion in tax leakage identified, instead of the full amount, realizing that severe penalties apply to unpaid, avoided or evaded taxes. This $40 billion annual figure means that we have $382 billion in savings and tax leakage/lost revenue from the existing system to put towards a decent UBI. This overshadows the cost of the NIT version of UBI put forth in the cost objection, and it surpasses the universal demogrant UBI cost Kesselman puts forward by over $30 billion (a $32 billion dollar surplus, without any personal income tax rises).

Third Response: *Freedom from Bureaucracy*

This response highlights the waste of bureaucracy entailed with numerous programmes that fail to achieve what a decent UBI can achieve in most cases.[25] It is a brief response that largely focuses on the real-life case of an individual experiencing multiple welfare bureaucracies. The complexity of this patchwork is overwhelming to individuals experiencing it directly. Sorting out all the bureaucracies and their costs is not worthwhile or necessary here. What is important is to convey this complexity and demonstrate that the costs of bureaucracy are often overlooked in the cost objection and not included in addition to the various programme costs it is associated with.

Monitoring people, co-ordinating hundreds of arbitrary and ever-changing rules, ensuring people are destitute first before qualifying for welfare or social housing adds excessive complexity to government. It also wastes a great deal of time and other resources on both sides of this divide. Potential recipients fill out many forms, travel to various offices, make appeals, get rejected and humiliated, try another process or programme. Bureaucrats – from the lowest ranking staff to the highest paid managers – could be engaged in much more productive and rewarding work.

Maintaining numerous offices, tribunals, employees and data control to carry this all out, micromanaging people's lives, costs a great deal of public money that is not sufficiently acknowledged in the cost objection. For example, we read about the cost of existing income assistance payments to individuals or families in the tens of billions, or the cost of building a social housing unit, or the maximum allowable monthly rent supplement in any jurisdiction. However, the bureaucratic cost is often excluded or ignored.

All this complexity is produced because people simply lack sufficient and stable income in most cases. An extended illustration from the Ontario Association of Food Banks is valuable here:

> Ali lived in subsidized housing as he grew up with his parents and younger sister and brother.

The family has been in Canada since 1994. Ali's family receives Ontario Disability Support Plan payments as his father is disabled. His mother works part time but makes very little. They came from the Refugee camps in Kenya. Ali...had a part time job since he was 17 and (as a child) none of his earnings reduced the family's ODSP payments. He was able to help a bit with household expenses from his earnings.

When Ali turned 18, the family lost the $105 or so monthly payments from the (exempted) federal Canada Child Tax Benefit. The family needed this money and Ali was able to make it up by getting more hours where he worked. (Laurie 2008: 29)

It became apparent that Ali was not going to be able to attend post-secondary school full time, not only because of a lack of savings and the loss of $105 monthly in child benefits, but because he needed a lot more income to pay for tuition and textbooks for college. He also learned that 50% of his net earnings of $600 a month would now be deducted from his father's disability payments. This because Ali was no longer considered a dependent child and was no longer in high school. The Housing authority then notified his parents that there would be a rent increase as a result of Ali being over age 16 and having graduated from high school, because he was not currently in school full time, and because he was making over $75 per month. The rent increase was $90 per month, effective immediately.

The decision to pursue post-secondary education part-time (instead of full-time) was made as a result of these cumulative income losses and bureaucratic programme features. Ali thought he may work additional hours to make up some of the income losses while studying only part-time. Financial assistance would still be required in the form of student loans by the Ontario School Assistance Program (OSAP). OSAP forms do not allow for consideration of Ali's circumstances, such as 50% of his net pay being deducted from his father's disability payments. OSAP officers told him to simply submit his application when he raised questions and concerns about these different factors he was encountering and how it would impact the size of his loan – they do not answer such questions.

At the end of the summer, Ali came to the reluctant realization that he could not remain at home with almost $300 of his net pay coming off his family's ODSP payment along with the $90 increase in rent. Like so many others in his situation, Ali moved out and established his legal residence at a friend's house. He became what is known by many public housing kids as a 'couch rider'.... (Laurie 2008: 29)

Couch riding while studying and working was not helping Ali's academic performance so he decided to give up his courses and look for another part-time job to combine with his existing job. At about this time he received a letter demanding his small OSAP loan be repaid with interest, his mother got a letter from "housing" stating that the family was now "overhoused" without Ali at home and they no longer qualified for their apartment. The family would have to leave (Laurie 2008: 29).

The story gets worse from there. Basic income at a decent level could help millions of people avoid all this arbitrary complexity and bureaucratic overlap. The negative life impacts that come with it are avoidable. Incurring all this bureaucratic overhead to make people's lives so miserable and difficult represents public funds that would be much better directed to UBI.

All these large bureaucracies also make government less transparent and therefore less accountable. It becomes exceedingly difficult to penetrate all their workings, and numerous opportunities for patronage and corruption arise (Montreal Gazette 2011; Alcoba 2013[26]). Better to have fewer bureaucracies operating at the highest levels of transparency, accountability and ethics than having public money scattered in too many conflicting directions.

This complexity has worsened since the early 1970s when guaranteed annual income/UBI was advocated in the Croll Report (Canada 1971). And from that government report four decades ago we could see the profligate waste of bureaucracy. "The cost of administering all this complexity is staggering... to issue one twenty-five-cent bus ticket, in terms of time and energy, cost the welfare system about four dollars!" (Canada, Croll Report 1971: 87). Already in 1971 the Croll Report was critical of "... innumerable welfare administrations and social-service organizations in Canada. The luxuriant growth of government and quasi-government agencies..." (Canada 1971: 67) which has only increased since then.

Without adding bureaucratic costs that are missed in the cost objection arguments our savings figures from implementation of UBI remain at $342 billion (Subsection "First Response: Savings from Replacement of Existing Income Security Programmes") plus $40 billion in tax losses from the existing system annually (Subsection "Second Response: Inefficiencies and Leakages in the Existing Tax System – No New Taxes!"). This $382 billion annual total stands against a $30 billion "cost" for a negative income tax version of UBI put forth by Kesselman, resulting in a $352 billion surplus/savings without any tax increases. The demogrant version of UBI is costed at $350 billion by Kesselman, resulting in a $32 billion savings/surplus from UBI implementation. And as stated, the cost of both versions of UBI is similar, with one version (demogrant) paying UBI upfront in monthly instalments and the other paying it as a negative income tax or "'top-up" at the end of the year. The demogrant will be paid back in part or in full by the end of the year depending on the income received by those in formal labour market employment (and depending on the amount of unearned income received by those in or out of formal market employment), as well as through consumption taxes and other taxes paid by those who had no income, or insignificant income, prior to UBI.

Bureaucratic costs add to these savings to be gained by UBI implementation. These bureaucratic costs are best calculated elsewhere due to constraints (time, resources, data availability and accessibility) and because they are not required to demonstrate the feasibility of UBI. One guiding point in this area of cost and savings worth emphasizing is the 16:1 ratio highlighted in the Croll Report above in terms of bureaucracy costs required to issue benefits in the form of one bus ticket. This is not necessarily the case with most welfare bureaucracy today, but we have all heard of charities that despite relying on large amounts of volunteer labour still often waste a large portion, or even the majority, of their financial contributions on administration and salaries. Public bureaucracy uses often well-paid staff and high-paid managers to execute the oppression detailed above, without volunteers (who would volunteer for such an awful task?). It is therefore not good policy to multiply bureaucracies or increase their size where it is not absolutely necessary and where cash payments/basic income can be far more effective.

*Fourth Response: **Externalities and Current Free-riding***

Dumping toxins in the air, land or water at little or no private cost leads to tremendous public costs. This occurs in the form of health costs. It can occur in the form of aesthetic damage, such as the death of diverse natural spaces used for recreation, which often earn public revenue. The loss of fisheries, or the loss of local food security due to polluted land, rivers or groundwater, can destroy local economies and necessitates often lower quality imports and expensive new infrastructure to make this feasible.

These are some examples and implications of ecological dumping. As David Suzuki (2008) and James Hansen (2009) have argued, exacting a proper levy on the use of the commons can mitigate such destructive activity and bring it down to a sustainable level while generating large revenues for a "green dividend" or green component to basic income.[27]

New forms of free labour being extracted from populations, especially younger demographics entering the workforce, in the form of unpaid overtime work, unpaid internships, excessive hours worked without premium pay previously associated with overtime, deliberate misclassification of employees as self-employed, etc. all represent social dumping (Perlin 2012; Pereira 2009; Standing 2009). Even more extreme versions of it involve the horrible vision of suicide nets placed outside the factory of mobile phone producer Foxconn (Trenholm 2012) as a twenty-first century solution to degrading labour. Offshoring of labour has led to incredible profits for corporations like Apple, which is directly linked to Foxconn, as they carry out social and ecological dumping simultaneously with such moves.

These externalities and free-riding have public costs, some of which UBI can help turn into savings. This response to the cost objection will explore some of these possibilities, starting with health costs incurred as a result of deteriorating labour conditions, which UBI can help rebalance. When faced with growing job and income precarity employees are less likely to speak up or confront such abusive conditions for fear of losing their income and their mortgaged homes, etc. UBI offers some ability to confront this degradation because a minimal, decent income is guaranteed. It may not be as high as your job income and it may not cover the expensive monthly payments on a large home and car, but it would always allow you to live in modest dignity and not miss a rent payment (or modest mortgage payment, or refinanced mortgage payment), and see you through a difficult patch for an extended time. This will allow many more people to voice important concerns that are currently silenced, and if the situation is unbearable they could eventually choose to leave rather than sacrifice their health (or commit suicide) if the employer fails to improve the situation.

No new taxation of labour income, or personal income tax increases, are required to achieve this generation of revenue, which can help protect the commons, improve the functioning of the economy and dramatically reduce public health costs. Curbing harmful financial speculation through modest levies has long been discussed for its great revenue generating capacity in contrast to the almost negligible size of such levies (beginning with Tobin tax and many possible variations of it). Ecological, social and speculation (financial, real estate and other) costs are often borne by the victims of these activities, with perpetrators externalizing these costs into the public realm – free-riding. Corporate subsidies (corporate welfare) is yet another version of this phenomenon. It recently cost global citizens trillions of dollars in the form of bailouts to banking, financial, auto and other corporations.

Starting with social-labour dumping that is continually intensifying, in the Canadian context alone we find $33 billion in annual health costs, or savings available (MacQueen 2007; Pereira 2009), if this situation were addressed. In the past this type of abuse was countered through strong labour movements at the national level. The labour movement has not provided a successful response to these recent challenges of deterioration, partly because of the dynamics of globalization. A UBI can mitigate a lot of this harm by empowering people with a minimal amount of control or say, and security, in their working lives, which does not currently exist (the majority of workplaces being non-unionized in Canada). This can provide an opportunity for new forms of collective response *and* for labour unions to become more relevant to desperate employees seeking an improvement in the labour market. Too many people have no hope or income security in confronting the challenges of rising stress, burnout and workplace disability associated with modern workplaces costing us $33 billion annually. "Stress is part of an explosion in workplace mental health issues" (MacQueen 2007), which is only intensifying with eroding income security.

Taking two-thirds of this $33 billion current cost, which is entirely avoidable, totals an additional $22 billion in indirect savings for UBI. One-third of this large amount is conservatively left in place to account for those who will continue to overwork themselves in pursuit of career objectives. But there is no reason why UBI cannot achieve better than this in restoring a healthy balance between work and life. Adding this amount to the total of $382 billion in available savings/revenue towards UBI implementation identified in Subsections "First Response: Savings from Replacement of Existing Income Security Programmes", "Second Response: Inefficiencies and Leakages in the Existing Tax System – No New Taxes!" and "Third Response: Freedom from Bureaucracy", results in $404 billion in accumulated savings/revenue thus far available, without increasing taxes on labour.

Continuing with externalities, dumping and free-riding that impose public costs on society that can be mitigated and recouped through fair-pricing, let us consider the ideas of leading environmental thinkers and practitioners David Suzuki and James Hansen (former head of NASA's Goddard Institute). Hansen (2009) argues a much more efficient and effective environmental proposal to address pollution and climate change than those currently on offer would be "fee and dividend" (carbon fee). His model based on usage of oil, gas and coal in the US in 2007 would yield $600 billion per year and result in a dividend for each adult American of $3,000 per year. David Suzuki (2008) as Canada's leading environmental thinker and personality sees even greater yields available in his modelling, while improving economic performance, sustainability and social well-being.

Taking one-tenth of the more conservative American figure above (approximate Canadian population relative to the US) can result in an additional $60 billion in financing for a green dividend or green component of UBI ($3,000 in additional UBI per adult). This has the simultaneous benefit of addressing urgent global, national and local environmental priorities. Adding this figure to the $404 billion in savings/revenue available to UBI totals $464 billion. A large surplus is created by applying this figure to any of the most pessimistic and simplistic of cost assessments/objections to UBI, whether considering the NIT or demogrant versions of the idea.

We can still consider much-needed speculation levies (on financial and land speculation), as well as corporate welfare giveaways before even needing to discuss personal income tax increases that the cost objection assumes is required from the outset. The surpluses demonstrated so far show that taxes on labour (labour market income) could even be cut.

Conclusion

Without raising any personal income taxes this study has shown that UBI is not too expensive to implement as a public policy. Savings from programme replacement and redundancy make up the majority of the rationale for this argument. Public universal health care as a cherished institution and programme has not been cut to achieve any programme savings or financing for UBI. Implementing UBI in fact helps improve the health system by reducing unnecessary burdens upon it. The financial surplus generated by implementing a UBI (in either negative income tax or demogrant versions) can actually lead to a personal income tax reduction if so desired.

Savings from bureaucracy have not been costed or calculated, which would only make the case for UBI even stronger. Other revenue-generating possibilities that do not include taxing labour, and which are non-controversial, such as taxing financial or land speculation have not been included in the net costing or financing of UBI here. A surplus is achieved by implementing UBI even without these additional non-controversial financing options.

Total savings of $342 billion (Subsection "First Response: Savings from Replacement of Existing Income Security Programmes") from redundant and/or ineffective programmes alone exceeds the Young and Mulvale cost of $21.5 billion for an NIT version of UBI (well over $300 billion in savings/surplus). As discussed, the NIT and demogrant versions of UBI, the latter having much higher costs attached to it in the cost objection argument, are not that dissimilar in terms of final cost.[28] The cost objection ignores the manner in which UBI is paid back in the demogrant version to arrive at a similar final cost to the NIT version.

Total savings (Subsection "First Response: Savings from Replacement of Existing Income Security Programmes") plus leakages in the existing tax system (Subsection "Second Response: Inefficiencies and Leakages in the Existing Tax System – No New Taxes!") largely from tax havens and practices carried out through them total $382 billion – far exceeding Kesselman's pessimistic costing of a demogrant version of UBI for Canada. Kesselman in his cost objection does not include any savings figures for UBI, nor does he address tax leakages and inefficiencies in the existing system that could be used to finance UBI. He simply jumps to the "need" to tax labour/personal incomes at "unacceptably" high rates to fund basic income. That has been proven false.

In the last two of four responses to the cost objection (Subsections "Third Response: Freedom from Bureaucracy" and "Fourth Response: Externalities and Current Free-Riding") I demonstrate how additional financing can be generated to further increase the surplus available by implementing UBI. These last two responses are only costed in a very limited manner and can generate far greater revenues. Thus, it is the existing welfare system and status quo with inefficient, often counterproductive programmes that is too expensive.

Appendix – Missed Savings and Redundancies in the UBI Cost Objection: A Summary

Young and Mulvale (2009) cost a "generous" UBI – enough to raise all Canadians out of income poverty – at $418 billion annually and find savings of $132 billion (leaving the Canada Pension Plan/Quebec Pension Plan untouched). This provides a net cost of $286 billion annually in their study, leading them to conclude UBI is financially out of reach. Kesselman (2013) costs UBI at $350 billion and provides no savings figures. Here are missed savings items that these studies failed to consider or cost to reduce the net cost (and even provide a surplus) for UBI. This is a summary of what is detailed in this study with a few additional items for consideration marked with an asterisk:

Item or programme	Missed savings (billions)	Missed savings subtotal
Additional tax revenue generation (at prevailing rates)	$86	
RRSP	$36.3	$122.3
TFSAs	$3	$125.3
Other tax shelters	$3	$128.3
Cost of poverty	$53	$181.3
Day care – partial redundancy	$9	$190.3
Social housing (and related programmes) – partial redundancy	$4	$194.3
Additional income assistance/welfare advocated in the cost objection (to status quo programmes)	$16	$210.3
WITB (EITC equivalent in the US)	Not costed[1]	
Special public employment projects advocated in the cost objection	Not costed	
Homeowner's Property Tax Grant	Not costed	
Charitable tax deduction programmes and government grants (food banks, poverty alleviation)	Not costed	
Corporate welfare-subsidy programmes	Not costed	
Sunshine list of excessive/high salaries in the public service*		
Total missed savings/redundancies	**$210.3**	
PLUS: tax leakage – current system		
Offshore tax havens/related evasion and tax avoidance	$40	$250.3
PLUS: bureaucracy savings		

(*continued*)

(continued)

Item or programme	Missed savings (billions)	Missed savings subtotal
Welfare elimination, social housing reduction, day care reduction, OSAP, etc.	Not costed	$250.3
PLUS: externalities/current free-riding		
Social-labour dumping, health costs	$22	$272.3
Green dividend/carbon fee	$60	$332.3
Tobin tax and/or variations at the national level (financial speculation levies)	Not costed	
Land speculation levy	Not costed	
Taxing *unearned income* at the same rate as earned income*		
Total missed savings, tax leakage (in current system) and new revenue from pricing externalities	**$332.3**	

[1] Estimates can be found in the Parliamentary Budget Office (PBO) – Bureau du Directeur Parlementaire du Budget report of May 27, 2014, "Revenue and Distribution Analysis of Federal Tax Changes: 2005-2013" pp. 18–20 (Fig. 6-2 demonstrates the annual increase in WITB payments to individuals and families since this federal program's inception in 2007). Approximately 9% of Canadian households received WITB benefits in 2014 according to the PBO. The EITC in the U.S. paid out $66.7 billion in tax year 2014 (Internal Revenue Service) with a 20% failure in the take-up rate - four out of five eligible recipients claiming this federal refundable tax credit: https://www.eitc.irs.gov/EITC-Central/abouteitc, Accessed 6 July 2016. "Determining eligibility for EITC is complicated" as indicated on the IRS website; the same being true for the WITB.

Adding this missed savings total (preventing externalities can also be considered savings, as this reduces public costs) to existing savings identified in Young and Mulvale (2009) of $132 billion, *totals $464 billion in savings* to be gained by implementing UBI.

Many items above have been costed partially or conservatively as explained throughout the chapter, leading to a greater potential for savings/surplus as a result of implementing a decent UBI. Several items have not been costed, leading to even greater savings than what is presented here.

NOTES

1. BC Teachers' Federation, "Historical Perspectives: The Canadian Centre for Policy Alternatives", January/February 2007 https://www.bctf.ca/publications/NewsmagArticle.aspx?id=10456.
2. Also, Canada's underground economy is valued at over $40 billion annually, not including illegal activities such as drug trafficking and prostitution, with

construction, finance, real estate, rental and leasing and holding companies making up the largest components of this unrecorded trade according to Statistics Canada (2014).
3. Thirty percent of $286 billion.
4. Clawback or supplemental tax back rates applied to UBI are not included here, and provide much higher net cost savings than 30%. Increasing amounts and forms of unpaid labour internationally (Perlin 2012; Pereira 2009) are also a problem UBI can mitigate, helping make currently unpaid (or underpaid) labour paid (or fairly paid) and thereby increasing personal income and income tax revenue. Other forms of taxes beyond income taxes are not taken into consideration by Young and Mulvale's footnote comment, which includes increased consumption and other taxes when people have a UBI as opposed to much smaller – or no – income currently. VAT rates in Europe are regularly well above 20% (European Commission 2014: 3). Combined federal and provincial sales taxes in Canada are usually between 12 and 15% (Munroe 2013).
5. Yalnizyan is referenced at the end of a CCPA article citing the $380 billion annual cost amount by a member of the CCPA (her own organization) by way of an update to the article in the "responses" section on March 3, 2014, and Yalnizyan points to Kesselman's work for justification. See Shaun Loney, "A Province with No Poverty," Policy Fix, *CCPA-MB*, February 28, 2014: http://policyfix.ca/2014/02/28/a-province-with-no-poverty/; Also, Reddit Canadian Politics, "I Am Armine Yalnizyan, Ask Me Anything," reddit.com, March 1, 2014: "I'm not a big fan of the minimum income a) huge cost...$380B for a liberating level of guaranteed annual income according to SFU economist Rhys Kesselman...I strongly recommend Rhys Kesselman's [sic] work on the guaranteed income". Yalnizyan provides a link to the same Kesselman *Inroads Journal* article cited in this chapter. In discussions with Glen Hodgson and Andrew Coyne, Yalnizyan reaffirms her support of Kesselman's work as the main objection to GAI/basic income (available online, February 1 2014, "I'm in Kesselman's camp on GAI").
6. And as we have seen with poverty-line income statistics (i.e. LICO) many multiple-person households will be far ahead of household poverty lines if recipients have an at-poverty-line UBI distributed per individual, because combined income households can extend incomes further. For example, a doubling of rent, mortgage or living space is not required if adding a second person to a household.
7. "Governments rely on a regressive tax structure as a source of public revenue. (Regressive taxes are those that take away a higher proportion of income from the low-income groups than from the high-income groups.)" Quote from Canada, Croll Report (1971: 46, or p. 74 of 241 in available

online versions of the Report). Numerous examples are given in the Croll Report of regressive taxation, many of which have been exacerbated since its publication decades ago.
8. www.tfsa.gc.ca.
9. As explained in the Financial Post (Heath 2011) "Rental real estate has been described by some as the equivalent of a super-charged RRSP".
10. There is no justification for *unearned* income to be taxed at a lower rate than *earned* income, and capital gains (outside of RRSPs) achieve this through a legislated 50% "inclusion" rate. This means only 50% of capital gains are subject to tax. This legislated limit has changed several times and was set at a 75% inclusion rate in Canada for a period in the 1990s (CBC 2012). All capital gains/unearned income should be treated as earned income is, that is, without special exclusions, and that is how I have treated capital gains with the removal of the RRSP programme. Sale of a principal residence is one exception where all capital gains taxation is excluded. There are certain *lifetime capital gains exemptions* whose existence and/or threshold amounts can be questioned, with additional revenues from such reduced exemptions being better directed universally to UBI. Overheated, volatile and sometimes corrupt stock markets and the companies in them should not be receiving such additional government promotion and incentives to encourage investment in them.
11. Eliminating the RRSP programme provides additional forms of government savings not explored here, representing additional revenue for UBI. For example, special RRSP tax credits for labour-sponsored investment funds means that each level of government provides an additional 15% in tax deductions (30% extra deductions from federal and provincial governments combined [FTQ 2014]). For each $1,000 invested your "investment only costs you $320!" as per the FTQ promotion. Labour-sponsored funds and associated organizations have been involved in major corruption probes in more than one province (Canadian Press 2014; Hopper 2012).
12. Writing about one category of tax shelters (not including RRSPs, TFSAs, RESPs, real estate, etc.), a tax lawyer specializing in non-profit and charity law states that philanthropic schemes "costs the Canadian governments billions of dollars per year" in tax incentives and tax receipts (Blumberg 2007).
13. If $132bn savings identified in Young and Mulvale's proposal is added to the $181bn in *missed savings* identified in this chapter, then Kesselman's less generous model of UBI is reduced in cost by $313bn, or 89%.
14. Putting children on a lower priority than that of servicing 24-hour/overnight gamblers represents an ethical new low, with government as facilitator of this anti-social conduct on both counts – providing the casinos (which many jurisdictions reject as anti-social) and then further enabling addictive

gambling behaviour by removing/treating children as obstacles and placing them in government-run "care" institutions. This is about as far from "care" (day, night or otherwise) as I have seen the term used. It is an abusive use of language and the comprehensive concept of care.

15. Mario Régis, head of the association of non-profit day care centres in Montreal, asks "How far do we want to go? We have to avoid a situation of abuse... children need their parents above all." He also points out the potential for employer abuse using these programmes to "take advantage of staff" (Peritz and Gagnon 2000).

16. The number of Canadians working "at two or more jobs or businesses almost quadrupled (from 208,000 to 787,000), compared with overall employment growth of 61%" from 1976 to 2003 (Statistics Canada 2004).

17. This is compounded by an extremely weak enforcement regime when it comes to workplace standards violations in Canada (Federal Labour 2006: 192–93, 220–21; Pereira 2009: 55–59). Pigg writes that the "stunning" increase in firings of pregnant women across Ontario is happening in all sectors and human rights advocates claim they have not seen this level of discrimination in two previous recessions and 30 years in the human rights field.

18. This reference [online] is not officially dated; however, it cites "Results of a national survey on housing conducted October 18–22, 2013." Accessed 22 May 2014.

19. Also see *Investment in Affordable Housing for Ontario: Program Guidelines*, August 2011, 20 (available in the CMHC source above). This money could be directly provided to Canadians as additional funding to UBI so that they could build their own homes, find their own existing homes for purchase or rental options without the restrictions of local and provincial housing authorities and their sometimes corrupt, expensive bureaucracies (Section 2, Subsection "Third Response: Freedom from Bureaucracy" will detail some of this corruption).

20. "Welfare programs don't have to remain as they are: they can be made less parsimonious..." (Kesselman 2013: Sect. 1). "For employable people on welfare, particularly singles, benefits are miserly to the point of almost requiring beggary and thievery for bare sustenance. These welfare benefits need to be increased..." (Kesselman 2013: Sect. 7).

21. For an explicit real-life example of how the existing welfare patchwork constantly creates new hardships for those caught in its numerous programmes (welfare, social housing and rent supplements, OSAP student loans, etc.), see Laurie (2008: 29–30).

22. Worth up to $500 each year for seniors 64 years of age or older who own a home in Ontario (see www.fin.gov.on.ca/en/credit/shptg/). This particular programme is an example of one that may justify partial redundancy with

a UBI in place, whereas many other programmes justify full redundancy/ elimination with all savings directed to UBI instead.

23. Adding a "clawback" to UBI can make the demogrant version even more similar in cost to the NIT version, depending on what rate the clawback is set at. Since there is such a large surplus to work with, the clawback could be set at a relatively low rate and still achieve a large surplus of public funds by implementing a UBI demogrant.

24. From their list of $132bn in savings I would start by removing the $14bn item for EI as discussed earlier (Subsection "First Response: Savings from Replacement of Existing Income Security Programmes"), as this programme should be retained as a contributory scheme. This would result in $118bn in savings from Young and Mulvale's figures, against a cost of $21.5 billion for UBI (NIT version), totalling $96.5bn in savings/surplus from implementing UBI.

25. Health care bureaucracy is not affected in this discussion. Again, the commitment in this thesis is to high-quality publicly delivered health care, with no intention of moving in the direction of private health care delivery as is commonly associated with the US.

26. "a damning report from the city's auditor-general that uncovered lavish employee expenses [at TCHC – Toronto Community Housing Corporation]. That probe also found staff repeatedly single-sourced contracts, sometimes without appropriate documentation, or split orders in order to get around procedures that would require board approval for big ticket items."

27. Some anti-ecological activities such as nuclear power and its waste generation need to be banned outright, as several countries and other jurisdictions have already done. Many toxic chemicals are also not needed in food or other products – organic food production could be pursued much more actively. However, destructive mining activities to produce luxury items and many other unnecessary consumer goods, for example, should have much higher prices attached to them to reflect this ecological harm, if local communities have accepted the mining activity. Excessively large vehicles (SUVs), sports vehicles (cars, boats, etc.) simply purchased as status items and burning excessive amounts of fuel are additional examples of items that should have a much higher "true-price" for the damage they cause to the commons and greater amount of resources required in their production, if society is to continue to accept their proliferation.

28. For additional support on this point see Pasma and Mulvale (2009: 2) in which they state: "Although the cost for the government's budget is greater than with an NIT, the end cost to taxpayers is not necessarily higher, since those with higher incomes pay the benefit back through their taxes. As well, the program may be cheaper to administer than an NIT because of the greater simplicity of its administration."

References

Alcoba, N. (2013) "Toronto Community Housing Hires Firm to Investigate kickbacks, Double Billing for Repair Work." *National Post*. 6 February.
Ariely, D. (2012) "Americans Want to Live in a Much More Equal Country (They Just Don't Realize It)." *The Atlantic*. 2 August.
Barry, B. (1996) "Real Freedom and Basic Income." *Journal of Political Philosophy* 4(3): 242–76.
BC Housing. (2010) "Rental Assistance Calculator" [online].
Blumberg, M. (2007) "Abusive Canadian Charity Tax Shelter Schemes." *Blumberg Segal LLP, globalphilanthropy.ca*. 23 November.
Buccheit, P. (2013) "16 Giant Corporations That Have Basically Stopped Paying Taxes – While Also Cutting Jobs!." *AlterNet*. 18 March.
Canada, Croll Report. (1971) The Senate of Canada. *The Report of the Special Senate Committee on Poverty: Poverty in Canada*. Ottawa.
Canada Without Poverty/Canada Sans Pauvreté. (n.d.) "The Cost of Poverty." Ottawa: CWP [online].
Canadian Labour Congress/Le Congrès du travail du Canada. (2013) "Child Care in Canada: A Scarce Resource." *Canadianlabour.ca*. 12 September.
Canadian Press. (2014) "FTQ wanted Pauline Marois to Help Stop Corruption Inquiry." 21 January.
Canadians for Tax Fairness. (n.d.) "Huge Cost of Tax Evasion Revealed as Campaign to Tackle Tax Havens Launches." *Taxfairness.ca*. Ottawa.
Capital Housing Region Corporation. (2011) *Direct Rent Supplement Program*. Edmonton: CRHC. 13 June. http://crhc.ca/media/66790/brochure_direc trentsupplement_130611.pdf.
CAW – Canadian Autoworkers Union. (n.d.) "Strong Pensions – Secure Future. Fact Sheet #2." *CAW/TCA*: http://www.caw.ca/assets/pdf/UPCFactSheet2.pdf.
CBC News. (2000) "Day-Care Centres to be Opened 24 Hours." 30 August.
CBC News. (2012) "Capital Gains Tax Break Falling Out of Favour." 29 March.
CBC News. (2013) "Retirement Savings in Canada – by the Numbers." 4 January.
Clinch, M. (2012) "Backlash as Starbucks UK Tax Avoidance Revealed." *CNBC/Reuters*. 16 October.
CMHC – Canada Mortgage and Housing Corporation (2014) "Affordable Housing Programs in Ontario" Ottawa: Government of Canada.
CPJ – Citizens for Public Justice (2012) "Bring our Tax Dollars Home." *CPJ.ca*. Ottawa. 16 November.
CRA – Canada Revenue Agency. (2014a) "Canadian Income Tax Rates for Individuals." http://www.cra-arc.gc.ca/tx/ndvdls/fq/txrts-eng.html.
CRA – Canada Revenue Agency. (2014b) "Offshore Tax Informant Program" [online].

Department of Finance, Canada. (2009) *Government of Canada Proposes Technical Changes Concerning Tax-Free Savings Accounts.* Ottawa: Government of Canada. 16 October. http://www.fin.gc.ca/n08/09-099-eng.asp.
Department of Finance, Canada. (2014) *Tax Expenditures and Evaluations 2013.* Ottawa: Government of Canada.
Dougherty, K, and A. Jelowicki. (2000) "Night Daycare to Make Debut." Reprinted in *Childcare Canada.* 31 August.
Emery, J.C., V. Fleisch, and L. McIntyre. (2013) *How a Guaranteed Annual Income Could Put Food Banks Out of Business.* Calgary: University of Calgary, School of Public Policy, Vol. 6, 37. December.
European Commission. (2014) *VAT Rates Applied in the Member States of the European Union.* ec.europa.eu/taxation_customs. 13 January.
Federal Labour Standards Review Commission. (2006) *Fairness at Work: Federal Labour Standards for the 21st Century.* Gatineau: Human Resources and Skills Development Canada.
Federation of Canadian Municipalities. (2013) "About the Housing Crunch." *Edmonton.ca/city_government/documents/ Housing_Roundtable_FCM_backgrounder.pdf.*
Forget, E. (2011). "The Town with No Poverty: The Health Effects of a Canadian Guaranteed Annual Income Field Experiment." *Canadian Public Policy – Analyse De Politiques* XXXVII(3): 283–305.
FTQ – Fédération des travailleurs et travailleuses du Québec. (2014) "Why Choose the Fonds RRSP?." *Fonds de solidarité FTQ.* online.
Gazette, Montreal. (2011) "Watchdog to Probe Quebec Daycare System." Reprinted in *Childcare Canada.* 2 December.
Hansen, J. (2009) "Cap and Fade." *New York Times.* 6 December.
Heath, J. (2011) "Real Estate: A 'Secret' Tax Shelter." *Financial Post.* 6 April.
Hermann, J. (2011) "Inside the World of London's 24/7 Interns." London Evening Standard. 8 August.
Hopper, T. (2012) "Manitoba Whistleblower Assigned to 'Non-job' after Warning of Government Fraud." *National Post.* 18 December.
Kesselman, J. R. (2013) "A Dubious Antipoverty Strategy: Guaranteeing Incomes for the Poor is Politically Unfeasible and Financially Unsustainable." *Inroads Journal* Winter/Spring: 33–43.
Krozer, A. (2010) *A Regional Basic Income.* Mexico City: United Nations – CEPAL.
Laurie, N. (2008) *The Cost of Poverty: An Analysis of the Economic Cost of Poverty in Ontario.* Toronto: Ontario Association of Food Banks. November.
Lee, M., and I. Ivanova. (2013) *Fairness by Design: A Framework for Tax Reform in Canada.* Vancouver: CCPA – Canadian Centre for Policy Alternatives, British Columbia. February.

MacQueen, K. (2007) "Dealing with the Stressed. Special Report: Workplace Stress Costs Us Dearly, and Yet Nobody Knows What It Is or How to Deal With It." *Maclean's*. 15 October.
Maloney, P. (2014) "What Is TCHC? Notes on a Scandal." Toronto Star. 22 April.
Milligan, K. (2012) "The Tax Free Savings Account: Introduction to the Policy Forum and Simulations of Potential Revenue Costs." *Department of Economics, University of British Columbia*. online.
Monsebraaten, L. (2013) "Ontario Affordable Housing Waiting Lists Still Climbing." *Toronto Star*. 12 November.
Morrison, M. (2013) "The Close: TSX Ends 2013 up Nearly 10 Per cent." *Globe and Mail*. 31 December.
Munroe, S. (2013) "Canadian Sales Tax Rates." *Canada Online*. 25 September.
OECD Family Database. (2013) "Public Spending on Childcare and Early Education." *Social Policy Division – Directorate of Employment, Labour and Social Affairs*. 29 July.
Pasma, C., and J. Mulvale. (2009) *Income Security for All Canadians: Understanding Guaranteed Income*. Ottawa: BIEN Canada.
Pereira, R. (2009) *The Costs of Unpaid Overtime Work in Canada: Dimensions and Comparative Analysis*. Athabasca University, MA Thesis.
Peritz, I, and L. Gagnon. (2000) "Tired of the Kids? Try 24-hour Daycare." *Childcare Canada*. 31 August.
Perlin, R. (2012) *Intern Nation: How to Earn Nothing and Learn Little in the Brave New Economy*. London: Verso.
Pigg, S. (2009) "Employers Fire Mothers-To-Be." *Toronto Star*. 24 April.
Québec. (2014) "Registering Your Child in Childcare Services (Day Care)." *Government of Québec*. 14 April.
Rainer, R. (2012) "Mr. Rob Rainer (Executive Director, Canada Without Poverty) at the Finance Committee." OpenParliament.ca. 31 May.
Rainer, R., and K. Ernst. (2014) "How Can We Not Afford a 'Basic Annual Income'?." *The Toronto Star*. 27 February.
Simms, D. (2013) "Charitable Giving Falling to Fewer Canadians." *CBC News – Business*. 21 February.
Standing, G. (2009) *Work After Globalization: Building Occupational Citizenship*. Cheltenham: Edward Elgar.
Statistics Canada. (2004) *Multiple Jobholding, by Sex and Age: Moonlighting Is Now More Common Among Women than Men*. Catalogue no. 71-222-XWE. 17 November.
Statistics Canada. (2007b) "Low Income Cut-Offs for 2006 and Low Income Measures for 2005." Income Research Paper Series, by Income Statistics Division, Ottawa: Minister of Industry: http://www.statcan.gc.ca/pub/75f0002m/75f0002m2007004-eng.pdf.

Statistics Canada. (2007a) *Economic accounts*: http://www41.statcan.gc.ca/2007/3764/ceb3764_000-eng.htm.
Statistics Canada. (2013) *Gross Domestic Product, 2006 – 2013*. CANSIM Table 380-0063: http://www5.statcan.gc.ca/cansim/a21.
Statistics Canada. (2014) "The underground Economy in Canada, 2011." 30 January: http://www.statcan.gc.ca/daily-quotidien/140130/dq140130c-eng.htm.
Suzuki, D. (2008) *Pricing Carbon: Saving Green. A Carbon Price to Lower Emissions, Taxes and Barriers to Green Technology* Vancouver: David Suzuki Foundation, prepared by M. K. Jaccard and Associates, EnviroEconomics.
Swanton, S. (2009) *Social Housing Wait Lists and the One-Person Household in Ontario*. CPRN – Canadian Policy Research Networks. January.
Taylor, P. (2007) "Everyone's Guide to Tax Shelters." *Money Sense*. December/January.
Ternette, N. (2012) "Guaranteed-Income Idea Kept Alive by Many." *Winnipeg Free Press*. 15 May.
TFSA – Tax-Free Savings Account. (2014) *Government of Canada*. http://www.tfsa.gc.ca/.
Trenholm, R. (2012) "Apple Factory's Wall-E robots and Suicide Nets Revealed." *Cnet.com*. 21 February.
Trudeau Foundation. (2013) *Responsible Citizenship: A National Survey of Canadians*. Montreal: The Pierre Elliott Trudeau Foundation, 31 October.
Van Parijs, P. (1995) *Real Freedom for All: What (If Anything) Can Justify Capitalism?*. Oxford: Clarendon.
Wadsworth, J. (2013) "Interns Death Puts Banking Culture Under Microscope." SFGate. 21 August.
White, S. (1997) "Liberal Equality, Exploitation, and the Case for an Unconditional Basic Income." *Political Studies* XLV: 312–26.
Young, M., and J. Mulvale. (2009) *Possibilities and Prospects: The Debate Over a Guaranteed Income*. Ottawa: CCPA – Canadian Centre for Policy Alternatives.

Richard Pereira is Doctoral Researcher at the University of Birmingham, UK, and was formerly an economist with the House of Commons in Canada.

PART 2

Cost Feasibility of Basic Income in Europe

CHAPTER 3

Financing Basic Income in Switzerland, and an Overview of the 2016 Referendum Debates

Albert Jörimann

Abstract This chapter attempts to determine the actual static cost of the introduction of a fully fledged unconditional basic income in Switzerland. The funding resources available for this policy initiative are also scrutinised. A "Clearing model" is presented in this work, and the share of social insurance benefits to be taken into account for the basic income (BI) amount is assessed. Options for covering the resulting gap are discussed, and an overview over the recent financing discussion in Switzerland is given.

Keywords Basic income · Unconditional basic income · Financing · Financing model · Gross cost · Europe

Switzerland has the honour of being the first country where a popular initiative has been submitted for a vote on the introduction of a basic income (BI). This is not difficult to achieve as Switzerland is the only country with an established tradition and practice of popular initiatives within its direct democratic system. Still, it was of the utmost interest to

A. Jörimann (✉)
Zurich, Switzerland

watch the clash of the opposing opinions and of the divergent social and economic interests during the voting campaign, where the financing question played quite an important role, as well as it does in other countries. I will summarise the most important developments within this context and will give some data for Switzerland.

Discussions about a BI scheme have come and gone in both political and scientific arenas since the 1980s. In Switzerland, several contributions were made in the middle of the 1990s, and in 2002, the Basic Income European Network (BIEN) Congress was organised in Geneva leading to the creation of BIEN Switzerland. This did not mean that there was a structured discussion of BI for the whole country, as BIEN-Switzerland in reality meant at that time above all BIEN-Geneva. This lasted until 2006 when a new impetus came from a new generation of anthroposophists based in Basel, which started discussions not only throughout Switzerland, but was active in Germany as well. This was the core of the new BI movement which in 2012 launched the collection of signatures for the popular initiative and handed over more than 126,000 signatures to the Federal Chancellery in the autumn of 2013.

In 2010 BIEN-Switzerland published a book about financing an unconditional BI with articles from Germany, France, South Africa and the UK as well as three articles from Switzerland (Le financement d'un revenu de base; BIEN Suisse 2010). Although the latter are relevant for my purpose, the other texts provided interesting insights into the different approaches of financing within Europe, both about the existing systems of social security and the methods themselves. The contribution of Pieter LeRoux of South Africa illustrated in a fascinating way how a BI system could be established in an emerging economy. The attempts of various groups to introduce a similar scheme in neighbouring Namibia, the obstacles and the pilot project in Otjivero, give further evidence of the paths of such proposals to introduce the system in a developing society and economy.

Part I: The Gross Cost

Preparations for the book revealed one thing – the cost of BI is easy to calculate according to the principle of one man/woman, one BI. Multiply the number of adult residents by the BI, the number of minor residents by 50% of the BI and add together. (For Switzerland in 2012 there were 6.6 mn adults and 1.46 mn minors aged under 18 years.) Obviously, the final total depends on the actual amount defined as the

Table 3.1 Gross cost of the basic income in Switzerland (2012)

Residents, adults (18 year +), 6.61 mn, CHF 30.000 pa	*198.3 bn CHF*
Residents, minors (−18 year), 1.43 mn, CHF 7.500 pa	*10.7 bn CHF*
Total: population of 8.04 mn	**209.0 bn CHF**

Source: Swiss Federal Statistical Office, Permanent resident population, Swiss Francs (CHF)

BI, as well as the definition of a minor (under age 21, 18 or 16). Some proposals even subdivide the amount allotted to minors, giving 50% BI to those between 10 and 20 years of age and 25% BI to those younger than 10 years. Usually, we speak of a monthly BI of €1,000 per adult/ €500 per minor for the two biggest neighbouring countries of Switzerland; France and Germany.

For Switzerland we propose an adult BI of CHF 2,500 (which at current foreign exchange rates, is more than double the French and German values, but this is another issue). For minors, contrary to the approach in our book published in 2010, we recommend a BI of CHF 625, (25% of the adult level) in line with the latest view of the promoters of the popular initiative. In all three countries, the sum of €1,000/CHF 2,500 is considered to be high enough to allow a single adult to have a decent standard of living without any luxury, but still be above absolute poverty (Table 3.1).

One remark as to how we arrived at this figure of CHF 2,500 per month for each adult. The Swiss Conference of Social Assistance (SKOS) calculated that one person needs approximately CHF 1,000 per month for basic needs (defined as food, clothing, energy, communication, transportation etc.), another CHF 1,000 per month for accommodation rental charges (this can vary depending on the local housing market), plus money to cover the medical charges that are not assumed by the cantons within their programme of subsidising health care insurance.[1] All in all, this adds up to something less than our figure of CHF 2,500. However, the BI is not intended as a programme to minimise expenditure for living costs. We believe that CHF 2,500 is an amount that can be argued as representing the "minimum that can be called decent".

The amounts can be related to a country's economic activity by comparing the BI costs to the Gross Domestic Product (GDP) (which makes sense because as well as making a fundamental change to the organisation of society today, the BI would also become an important element of the overall national economy). In both Germany and France in 2014, the gross cost of BI would more or less equal one-third of GDP (Germany GDP €2,735.80 bn/BI between €880 and €885 bn; France GDP €2,113.8 bn, BI €709 bn). The figures for Switzerland more or less confirm the ratio, with GDP of about CHF 600 bn and BI about CHF 209 bn.

If we further assume that about two-thirds of GDP consists of salaries on the production side and two-thirds of domestic consumption on the spending side (the other third encompassing investments, etc.), we have quite a precise picture of what the BI is supposed to mobilise within developed countries. In emerging and developing countries, the proposal will have a different make-up.

It is obvious that the reshuffling of such amounts within the economy and society in general would create a whole range of political debate and action, as it would activate all instruments of the political theatre. The left wing would try to finance the BI by raising the taxes of the rich and introducing levies on capital gains. The neoliberal side would try to abolish the traditional social security and protection system and replace it with a BI that would barely cover the cost of food and housing. Alongside these positions, one would find a universe of proposals to redefine the tax system; for example, by abolishing all income tax and replacing it with a value-added tax (VAT) of 100% (an idea proposed by the German entrepreneur and anthroposophist Goetz Werner in 2007) or by financing the whole BI by levies on energy. Generally speaking, more or less every interest/pressure group would try to strengthen its position within the distribution process during the introduction of a BI (as is the case with every other attempt to change any element of modern society and the state – in my view the main reason why modern states tend to be rather inert).

These political and ideological controversies are inevitable. Now before they start in earnest, we have to know what they are all about. First, we have to calculate how much the introduction of BI in Switzerland would cost *at current value*, that is, by replacing what can be replaced without changing the current system of social insurance/social security – and furthermore by compensating the BI payment with salaries above a certain, *decent* level which, I hope would be the case for the majority of salaries, at least in Switzerland.

Part II: The Clearing System

As a matter of fact, the following "clearing" model is based on the assumption that every person earning an average income would finance their BI themselves. This assumption by the way is also valid for other models, although they use different, indirect models of compensation, mainly within the taxation system. In my proposal, I am talking about a clearing payment that does not leave space for any misuse of tax income that would have been levied for one purpose and afterwards be employed for another. It is a direct, personal "refunding" of the BI, which is levied on the salary and paid by the employer to the BI Fund. Full clearing/repayment starts at a level somewhat higher than the BI amount which I have proposed for two reasons: (1) the BI is a real *basic* income and should not be considered as a target value at any socio-economic level. Full reimbursement starting at the level of the BI itself would establish it as such a target value. (2) Practically all who deal with the situation of low and basic incomes state that it is essential that individuals maintain the potential to develop additional financial activity on top of a basic income. Therefore, a clearing scale should be adjusted accordingly and start with the full clearing on a level beyond the BI.

This clearing system is to my knowledge, the simplest and most radical approach to establish a purely static evaluation of what BI would really mean in supplementary costs. In addition, we have to propose a scheme which allows both of these revenue sources (clearing payments and transfer of existing social benefits) to be used to finance the BI. This is what we did during the development of the clearing model. It is obviously tailored for the specific Swiss circumstances, but could easily be adapted to other situations. As said before, the clearing system leaves everything unchanged in the first step. The contributions from salaries to the old age pension (AHV), invalidity insurance (IV), accident and unemployment insurances continue to be levied, and the respective budget positions of the federal state, the cantons and municipalities are maintained and redirected to the BI Fund. (In Switzerland, the cantons and municipalities are the main recipients of direct taxes and social aid is the responsibility of the municipalities.)

Clearing Payments and Scale

In order to make the system work smoothly, a system needed to be developed to allow increases in income for those with lower monthly salaries (in our view less than CHF 4,000 per month). Without this, there would be no incentive to improve performance (and therefore pay) at the lower salary levels and it avoids any income traps for those whose income could increase, for whatever reason. People obviously should not be punished for their efforts, above all in the sensitive area of low, "sub-decent" income. (Some people in this category are part-time working partners of those with a full income – but this is another story.) The scale we established is shown below (Table 3.2).

The approach for implementing this scheme in Switzerland was to follow the most important institution within the social security system – the mandatory public old age pension scheme. This is not only well established with an excellent reputation among the whole population but also already covers all residents in the country (including children), so that on the administrative/technical level nothing needed to be re-created or changed.

Table 3.2 Earned income/month with BI at CHF 2,500/month and clearing payment scale

Income/ month before BI A	Basic Income B	Clearing percentage C	Clearing amount D (B × C)	Effective variation E (B – D)	Income/month after clearing payment F (A+E)
CHF	CHF	%	CHF	CHF	CHF
50,000	2,500	100.0	2,500.00	0	50,000.00
10,000	2,500	100.0	2,500.00	0	10,000.00
5,000	2,500	100.0	2,500.00	0	5,000.00
4,000	2,500	100.0	2,500.00	0	4,000.00
3,500	2,500	86.5	2,162.50	337.50	3,837.50
3,000	2,500	73.0	1,825.00	675.00	3,675.00
2,500	2,500	59.5	1,487.50	1,012.50	3,512.50
2,000	2,500	46.0	1,150.00	1,350.00	3,350.00
1,500	2,500	32.5	812.50	1,687.50	3,187.50
1,000	2,500	19.0	475.00	2,025.00	3,025.00
500	2,500	5.5	137.50	2,362.50	2,862.50
300	2,500	0	0.00	2,500.00	2,800.00
0	2,500	0	0.00	2,500.00	2,500.00

Source: Le financement d'un revenue de base inconditionnel. Zurich: Seismo 2010

The AHV old age pension scheme is often cited as a kind of a BI for the retired, which is largely, but not entirely correct (but this, again, is another story). The application of this scheme to the statistical realities of the Swiss economy would produce an amount which is transferred directly from salaries to a BI account – the former Old Age Pension Scheme now obviously becoming the BI Fund (some 38 bn. CHF, see Table 3.4 below). It should be stated upfront that for Switzerland, the calculation appears to be relatively easy because a large majority of the population is employed, producing a relatively concise picture of the income landscape (Table 3.3). In other countries where there are large proportions of self-employed or black-market workers, this approach would be difficult.

Nevertheless, we have to work with some assumptions, since the indications differ according to the statistical base used (Beschäftigungsstatistik (Schweiz), Job Statistics (BESTA), Federal Statistical Office, etc.) and do not give clear indications for some aspects that would be important for a correct evaluation of the situation, for instance like the level of employment, etc.

Table 3.3 Income classes in Switzerland (2010)

Gross annual income	Full time	Workforce (2,836,000)	Part time	Workforce (1,474,000)	Total	Workforce (4,310,000)
CHF	%		%		%	
0	0.3	8,508	2.0	29,480	0.9	38,900
0–26,000	2.1	59,556	34.3	505,582	13.5	581,000
26,001–52,000	11.2	317,632	29.7	437,778	17.7	762,870
52,100–78,000	32.0	907,520	15.5	228,470	26.2	1,129,220
78,001–104,000	21.9	621,084	6.3	92,862	16.4	706,840
104,001 +	22.7	643,772	3.1	45,694	15.8	680,980
No indication	9.9	280,764	9.2	135,608	9.6	413,760

Source: Federal Statistical Office, table je-d-03.04.00.01.xls

Table 3.4 Clearing payment

Income class and clearing payment (2010)	CHF (bn)
About 620,000 earn less than CHF 26,000/year (2,167/month) Assume a clearing payment percentage of 20% of BI Calculation 620,000 × CHF 2,500/month × 12 × 20%	3.70
Assume 650,000 earn between CHF 26,000 and CHF 48,000/year (2,167–4,000/month) Assume a clearing payment percentage of 70% of BI Calculation 650,000 × CHF 2,500/month × 12 × 70%	13.65
The balance of 3,060,000 people earn above CHF 48,000/year Clearing payment percentage is 100% of BI Calculation 3,060,000 × CHF 2,500 × 12 × 100%	91.80
Total sum of clearing payment, based on 2010 workforce	109.15

To calculate the clearing amounts we have to make several broad assumptions to bring together the data from the above two tables (Tables 3.3 and 3.4) as follows:

Table 3.4 is based on figures from 2012 so the 2010 sum needs to be adjusted in line with the growth of the workforce from 2010 to 2012. Assuming this is in line with the general population increase of 2%, the 2010 total needs to be increased by 2% resulting in a total sum of the clearing amount for 2012 to be *CHF 111 bn.*

Then, it is generally agreed that the parts of the social security or social insurances that cover the basic needs are to be put into the service of the BI. This means for example that for jobless benefits, only the parts corresponding to the basic amount can be transferred to the BI financing. (In Switzerland, the aim of the jobless benefit is to guarantee a certain standard of living for a limited time, usually two years, so the income is in practice higher than the BI.) In Table 3.5 below, we have detailed which amounts of the national accounts on social security and the different social insurances we would take into account for the BI budget.

There are several other items of state expenses at all levels that can be added to this figure, for example, part of the agriculture subsidy relevant to the farmer's salaries, scholarship funds, minor subsidies and aids under various titles and obviously economies at the administrative level. We do not suppose that they will be much higher than 5 bn.

Table 3.5 Social insurances, total expenses and part of expenses creditable to the BI account

Title of programme	Operative expenses	part creditable to BI	Amount
	CHF		CHF
Old age pension AHV	38.6 bn	100%	38.6 bn
Invalidity insurance	7.4 bn	Pensions (app. 80%)	6.2 bn
Complementary benefits	4.4 bn	50%	2.2 bn
Accident insurance	5.8 bn	Pensions, creditable to B.I. 30% (est.)	2.0 bn
Military service and maternity	1.6 bn	100%	1.6 bn
Jobless insurance	5.1 bn	50%	2.6 bn
Child benefits	5.3 bn	100%	5.3 bn
Social assistance	4.1 bn	100%	4.1 bn
Total			**62.3 bn**

Source: various statistics and editions of the corresponding offices and insurances, notably Pocket statistics of the Social Insurances in Switzerland 2014

Health care is usually considered as an important part of the social insurance system. In Switzerland, it is mandatory as in most other countries, but the contributions are paid by the individual and cost between CHF 400–500 per month per adult. A good half of the population (e.g. far more than those regarded as poor) receive canton subsidies for these expenses. Because this would somehow exceed the considerations in the context of the substitution for the BI Fund, we have left this aside.

Coming to the abolition of a large part of the bureaucratic structures of social assistance and social insurance (a long-term desideratum of the liberals), we confirm for Switzerland that part of the administration would disappear, mainly at the federal and cantonal level. We would expect fewer economies at the municipal level where the practical social work is done, since the introduction of BI would not solve all the problems of the people from one day to another. It might even be that during a certain period, more human resources would be needed to support and guide those who otherwise have been monitored (at least marginally) during their periodic visits to the municipal offices.

Thus, the sum that can be transferred from the existing social security system (and several minor other items) to the BI Fund is at current value and for the year 2012, about CHF 68 bn. Adding the CHF 111 bn from the clearing payment calculation, we arrive at a global amount of money which can be transferred from existing systems to the fund to be CHF 179 bn. The gap between this and the calculated gross cost of CHF 209 bn is about CHF 30 bn per year.

Part III: How to Cover the Gap

Now we have reached the frontier of the cost neutrality by maintaining all elements as they actually are. We have calculated that there is a gap of CHF 30 bn between the cost of our proposal giving full coverage to all 8 mn residents (BI of CHF 2,500 per month for adults and CHF 625 for those under 18) and the amount of funds which could be raised from the current system.

From this point on, controversy starts as it is not obvious how to finance the annual deficit of CHF 30 bn and to direct the additional money to the BI Fund. For each adult person, the deficit amounts to nearly CHF 4,500 per year, which is approximately CHF 400 per month. It is clear that we cannot levy this sum directly from the resident population as this would simply correspond to a reduction in the BI, and we have already defined the amount of CHF 2,500 per month to be the minimum that can be called a "decent" payment.

There are mainly three technical possibilities to fill the gap – taking money from earned income, redirecting funds from other sources or printing more money.

We excluded printing money at the very start of our investigation, which may come as a surprise since the printing of money is nowadays the macroeconomic measure par excellence and, if money is god, it is the real "deus ex machina" of national and international economic policy. For us, printing money is not an option at this stage.

Redirecting funds from other sources to the BI Fund could be achieved by taxing capital flows or gains or revenues and, particular only to Switzerland, using private insurance funding as follows: in 2025 the 40-year period of initial funding of the so-called second pillar (mandatory occupational pension plans, as opposed to the first pillar, the mandatory public pension plan respectively the AHV cited above) will expire, which means that the CHF 10–20 bn per year foreseen to build up capital during these 40 years (1985–2025) will become obsolete and therefore, in some way will become freely available. (According to the "Pocket statistic of social insurance 2015", in 2012 the statutory occupational pension system collected CHF 63.5 bn in contributions and spent in the same period CHF 47.5 bn.) From a political/ideological point of view, this money "belongs" equally to the employees and employers. From a macroeconomic point of view, the money will become a "useless" surplus that will enhance neither consumption nor investment spending and would just build another barrel of liquidity into the ocean of global capital markets. Redirecting the cash to the BI Fund would be a far more reasonable measure than letting it disappear into the shadow of general accounts. The balance between wages, profits, prices and savings will not be changed basically by either way of proceeding.

The third possibility is to consider taking the corresponding amounts from the pot of earned income, and the two main instruments in how to achieve this are direct and indirect taxes. The originators of the popular initiative from Basel favour the indirect tax route in line with the German entrepreneur, billionaire and anthroposophist Goetz Werner, who in 2006 urged the replacement of every direct tax by indirect taxes, raising VAT from 20% (in Germany) to 100% which would cover not only the needs of the BI but also the rest of the state's expenses as well.

Value-Added Tax

Werner's main argument is that all taxes, including direct tax, are ultimately reflected in the price of products anyway, so having just one tax at the end of the production-life cycle of goods, that is, at the point of sale, would be a logical and efficient form of taxation. (This argumentation is still maintained the promoters of the popular initiative, Daniel Häni and Enno Schmidt and their "Initiative Grundeinkommen" in Basel with their so-called Latte-Macchiato-These.[2]) Such a system has got two other major advantages, at least for entrepreneurs and billionaires. Firstly, it abolishes any taxation of what is always considered to be the raison d'être of every enterprise, that is, the earnings and the distribution of profits to the shareholders. Secondly, abolishing income tax puts an end to the principle (fixed for example in the Swiss Constitution) that every person has to contribute to the cost of the community as a whole (society) according to his/her economic capability. It is obvious that the wealthy would pay more VAT due to their higher level of purchasing, but this would in no way be comparable to the actual level of income tax, even if it were levied at a flat rate. (Actually, instead there is usually a considerable progression of the tax rate for rising revenues; with a sole rate of VAT without direct tax payments their tax duties would become sharply regressive.)

In the meantime, Goetz Werner has revised his proposal and now suggests only a partial hike of VAT, as do his followers in Switzerland (see their model below), and indeed, indirect taxation is a valid instrument for consideration. In Switzerland, VAT in its current form (basically 7.8%) brings in about CHF 3 bn per percentage point (with three different rates and numerous exceptions). Thus, to cover the financial gap of the BI with VAT alone, you would have to raise the rate by 10% to about 18%, which at first glance does not seem too ambitious when compared with the neighbouring countries' rates of about 20%. Still, such a rise would mean a massive intervention into the political speculation potential and thus in the balance of political interests, VAT being the most important source of income for the federal authorities, "ex aequo et bono" with the federal direct income tax from natural and legal persons. But the redirecting of such amounts leads to massive battles around the balances of political interests. VAT itself can probably provide only a part of the financing of the gap we have calculated. The technical advantage of VAT would be that the decided increase would be possible without further difficulties and without other than expected consequences: when VAT rises, some sectors/goods and services manage to pass on these increased costs to the customers and others don't – but that is quite normal.

It might still appear interesting that Goetz Werner says in his last contribution to the German Internet newspaper "Spiegel online" that, at actual rates for Germany, a BI would be located at the start in the area of the existing Hartz-IV-payments (about 600 €/person/month), therewith matching the calculations done several years ago by the research team around the former Prime Minister of the German Bundesland Thüringen, Dieter Althaus.[3]

Other Indirect Taxes – Energy Taxation

There are other indirect taxes which can be considered, such as levies on alcohol and tobacco and on energy consumption. Within the context of climate change and ecological issues generally, energy taxation is one of the major subjects in the political debate. This kind of indirect taxation is special insofar as it does not only have an influence on energy consumption (as is intended) but also touches several industrial sectors whose energy consumption is above the average. These will claim tax exemptions because otherwise they risk having to close down factories, as well as eventually the energy producers themselves because of a tendency of falling revenues. In the first place, it will affect the consumer, again sparing those who have relatively high incomes but supporting the goal of reducing energy consumption, of course. Energy taxation is more or less a VAT on specific goods. It depends very much on the political will of parliament and the people if such funds could be considered for the financing of a BI.

According to the BFE/Federal Office of Energy 2013, the global energy consumption in Switzerland is around 255 bn kWh. Therefore, financing the entire gap of CHF 30 bn with an energy tax would cost about 12 cents per kWh.

Direct Taxes

Before starting the proper discussion, it must be stressed that direct taxation is one of the most important elements of "passive exportation" in Switzerland. With its moderate, if not low taxation level, the country attracts both people and investments from all over the world, not any more the "dirty" money that Swiss banks have been accused of laundering for decades, but just the normal wealth that finds these conditions very welcoming and which in turn allows the tax rates to remain low – a logical consequence of the concentration of good tax payers within this small space in the Alps. Thus, Switzerland attracts some of the so-called tax substrate (the tax base) from other countries; on the other hand, it is logical that any larger intervention can have important consequences on the said tax substrate. Both capital funds and the rich are shy and fugitive.

Another particularity is that the lion's share of the income tax goes to the cantons and municipalities, as I have mentioned above. This may be an additional reason for the relatively low tax rates, since at the communal level, democratic decisions about tax rates tend to be strict and severe, and the control close to the establishment of projects which are often subject to popular votes and the budget – and finally the tax payment. Additionally, there is nowadays fierce competition amongst the cantons to attract the wealthy tax payer. As an example, some years ago the canton of Obwalden tried to introduce degressive tax rates for the rich which was ultimately prohibited by a ruling of the Supreme Court of Switzerland. Still, the race for the rich goes on at full speed leading more and more cantons to cut budgets and expenditure. (In 2010 the Swiss central state, the Confederation spent about CHF 60 bn [of which CHF 18 bn was transferred to the cantons]. CHF 22 bn was financed by direct taxes [CHF 9.879 bn from individuals]; the cantons spent CHF 75 bn, collecting CHF 39 bn in direct taxes [CHF 28 bn from individuals] and paying CHF 5.5 bn to the municipalities.[4] The municipalities spent CHF 43 bn, of which CHF 19 bn stemmed from individual direct taxation. This means that on all three levels of government, individual direct tax brought in about CHF 56 bn to the treasury.)

It would be difficult and above all illogical to try to finance the BI gap by taxes at the cantonal or municipal level; already transferring some of the expenses of cantons and municipalities (e.g. social assistance) to the BI Fund will require some ingenuity. Thus only income tax at the federal level can be used to levy the necessary amounts, or indeed one can introduce a separate/special federal tax, a kind of a BI Tax over and above the federal income tax with a contribution sizing of its own. For logical and systematic reasons, this would be a very clean and transparent solution without mixing up all kinds of different issues. Here again, financing the entire gap of CHF 30 bn by an additional direct federal tax would require an increase of 50% if the whole tax base of CHF 22 bn was used, or by 200% if only the earned income of individual earners was taken into account (CHF 10 bn). Among the questions that would arise, the first would be whether the BI should be taken into account for the calculation of the tax base. In this case, the BI would become a part of the tax base for those who do not refund their BI within the clearing system. For the others, there would be no imminent change, the BI clearing payments being deductible from the taxable sum. In order to exempt the BI from taxation (which is a logical thing to do), the tax-free threshold would have to be increased to the amount of the BI. Based on figures from the 2011 taxation year, this would cause losses of some CHF 40 mn, a sum not relevant for our considerations.

Currently, the direct federal tax allows relatively high tax-free amounts. For instance in 2014, the tax-free amount is CHF 14,500 CHF for singles and CHF 29,300 for couples. Then there are tax-free sums for professional expenses (around CHF 5,000), a special exemption of CHF 13,400 if both in a couple are working, another exemption of CHF 6,740 for private pension plans and obviously an exemption for children of CHF 6,300 per child. Thus, a single person could claim a tax-free amount of up to CHF 20,000 per year and a married couple with 2 children, up to CHF 50,000 per year. Furthermore, the tax rates up to the middle-income levels are quite modest, so that an increase as described would not significantly affect the tax payment and therefore the tax revenue.

The following calculations are still approximations, not because of the increase of the tax-free threshold, but because of the current system based on the taxation of couples instead of individuals, whereas individual taxation forms the base of our entire considerations in accordance with the principle of the BI being paid unconditionally to everyone. The payment of an individual and unconditional BI would anyway entail a revision of the tax system at some future time, abolishing the taxation of couples and replacing it with the subsequent levying of taxes of individuals only (thereby satisfying an old request of parts of the liberal wing as well). But for the argumentation in this chapter, we try to work with the "distorted" figures of individuals and couples as well as possible.

Let us have a look at the picture that would result. According to Table 3.3, out of a workforce of 4.310 mn people, approximately 750,000 earned less than CHF 30,000 per year (approx. 620,000 people earning up to CHF 26,000 per year plus a sixth of those in the next band up to CHF 52,000 per year). That means that 3.6 mn people, the balance of the workforce, would in this scenario need to cover the CHF 30 bn gap by income tax alone, giving a per capita contribution of some CHF 8,500 per year/CHF 700 per month, which is obviously too high, especially for those with lower incomes. Even when trying to weigh the contribution according to the income level the results are somewhat shocking. Table 3.6 below shows a hypothetical range of

Table 3.6 Hypothetical model for additional income tax for incomes above CHF 30,000 per year

Gross annual income	Total employed	Contribution range per month	Average contribution per month/year	Result
CHF 30,000 – 52,000	650,000	CHF 30 – 300	CHF 200/2,400	CHF 1.5 bn
52,000 – 78,000	1,130,000	300 – 600	400/4,800	5.4 bn
78,000 – 104,000	707,000	600 – 900	700/8,400	6.0 bn
104,000 +	681,000	900–5,000	1,000/12,000	8.0 bn
Total	3,168,000			*20.9 bn*
No indication	413,760		700/8,400	3.5 bn

contribution considered for each band, together with an average contribution used to calculate the results. The total of CHF 20.9 bn is still only two-thirds of the gap. We can add some CHF 3.5 bn for those who have not indicated which band they are in, but this is purely speculative.

This shows that covering the financing gap of CHF 30 bn exclusively by direct federal taxation is technically possible, but in practice not really feasible because the additional income tax would be quite high for the middle-income earners. A steeper progression might help, but we would then be at risk of damaging the whole construction of the direct federal taxes where the wealthy pay substantially more than the middle-income earners, and the lower-income earners pay no tax at all.

So, it is clear that only a part of the gap of CHF 30 bn could be financed by additional income taxes. And not to be ignored is that for the time being, the Swiss Constitution fixes a maximum tax rate for high incomes of 11% which would be exceeded with this proposal – but these aspects are rather secondary in view of the whole change proposed.

Part IV: The Models in Discussion

In our book *The financing of a Basic Income* (BIEN-Suisse, 2010) we have presented three models for Switzerland of which one is the clearing model at the centre of this article. The other two models are from Bernhard Kündig, Vice President of BIEN-Switzerland in 2010, and Daniel Häni and Enno Schmidt, co-founders of the Initiative Grundeinkommen, the driving force behind the start of the popular initiative.

Bernhard Kündig

In addition to the substitution of existing social security payments, Bernhard Kündig proposes the replacement of the duties/contributions on the salaries that finance the social security programmes by a so-called social VAT of about 23%. VAT would be the main financing source of the BI and would be used only for this purpose. All the services of the public administration and public enterprises would be exempt from VAT. In addition, he urges the reform of income tax by replacing it with a flat tax of 22.5% with a high tax-free threshold, abolishing the large majority of possible tax deductions. This would cover the remaining financial needs of the BI Fund as well as the normal expenses of the Confederation.

Häni and Schmidt

As I have mentioned earlier, Häni and Schmidt advocate in principle a solution based on VAT, arguing much like their mentor Goetz Werner that the different taxes an enterprise has to pay end up in the price of the goods sold anyway (and ignoring like Goetz Werner profit or wealth taxation, etc.). As I have done in this article, in practice they advocate the transfer of existing social security payments into the BI Fund, as far as it is appropriate to transfer them. Their numbers in this context are very much the same as the numbers in this article. Furthermore, they propose some compensation with salaries as I have presented above. However, they do not foresee any particular mechanism to provide this compensation but leave the development to the forces of the labour market (with some assumptions that do not exactly correspond to the price building mechanisms of an average labour market, but this is not that important). Finally, they achieve similar figures as in this article for the compensation effect, for the replacement of social security payments and for the gap that would have to be covered. They give no concise solution as to how to fill the gap, because in their eyes, it is far more important to understand the principle of the BI than to provide the details of a financing regime that anyway would be overthrown in the political process. Consequently, the main promoters of the popular initiative the popular initiative do not give specific indications about these questions, starting with the amount itself; the text of the popular initiative only states "...the financing and the amount of the BI is governed by the law".[5] At this very stage of the public discussion, I think this was a wise thing to do.

Müller and Straub

During the launch of the initiative, two other promoters of the popular initiative, Christian Müller and Daniel Straub published a booklet entitled "Die Befreiung der Schweiz" (The Rescue of Switzerland; Limmat Verlag, Zurich 2012) with the following estimates: gross cost CHF 200 bn covered by CHF 128 bn transferred from earned income and CHF 70 bn from existing payments of the social insurances/social security, leading to a financing gap of CHF 2 bn. The difference to our estimates concerning transfers from earned incomes stems mainly from the fact that they did not use a scalable "clearing" but instead calculate with full reimbursement/transfer from the very first franc above the BI amount. Otherwise, it seems obvious that they have overestimated the potential transfers of the actual social security into the BI Fund.

Müller and Straub II, Analysis of Potential

Several authors have dealt with the economic potential of the introduction of a BI; Müller and Straub have published during the voting campaign such an analysis in the form of a pre-study within their "Institut Zukunft" (Institute of the Future), calculating the positive effects as follows: the positive effects on mental and physical health are estimated at 13 bn CHF, the increase of output productivity at 31 bn CHF, additional consumption at 8.7 bn CHF, together with other minor factors a one-off contribution of about 55 bn CHF. The sustainable potential (from the reduction of income inequality and an increase of the creation of enterprises, is estimated at some 4 bn CHF.[6] To be frank, I am not convinced of the reliability of these numbers and therefore cannot take them into account for the financing debate.

Others

In the course of the campaign for the popular initiative, various other attempts and proposals have been given birth, including a micro-taxation of financial transfers or a mix of the systems mentioned above, according to the creative potential of the respective authors. It is not the aim of this article to discuss these valuable contributions, since they have not yet matured into a coherent form, which might very well succeed in the months to come.

In Comparison: A Schematic Proposal

A simple and illustrative mechanism of how financing BI could work within the taxation of earned income, not specifically in Switzerland, but in every country, is one of the models presented by the German party "Die Linke". According to this proposal, every single earned Euro would be taxed at a rate of 30%, in linear or flat tax form. (It could also be slightly progressive taxation, or linear, but at a higher rate, or even at a higher rate and progressive.) Instead, the BI (financed by these direct and/or other indirect taxes) would be paid tax-free alongside the earned income of everybody. This mechanism has been presented before, for instance in the 1990s by Philippe Van Parijs (Real Freedom For All, Oxford 1995, Clerendon Press), and I think this model captures the financial/technical essence of the BI scheme very well in a systemic form.

Part V: The Opponents

After the work "Solidarität neu denken" of Martino Rossi and Elena Sartoris in 1996, there were practically no further publications dealing explicitly with the financing of a BI. In 2004 and 2005, Christoph Schaltegger and Michael Gerfin/Robert E. Leu[7] discussed the introduction of tax credits respectively of a negative income tax, and Tobias Müller presented a model of a participation income, mainly dealing with the possible effects on the labour market in Switzerland.[8] Otherwise, the book of BIEN-Switzerland in 2010 about the financing was the first attempt to visualise the financial side of the BI proposal.

Since the launch of the popular initiative, two reactions from opponents of the BI were published, presenting more or less detailed calculations.

Economiesuisse

Six months after the start of the collection of signatures for the BI popular initiative in 2012, the Swiss entrepreneurs' Public Relations (PR) organisation Economiesuisse published an article on the BI.[9] The arguments were presented under the sarcastic title: "A BI?—Unfortunately not", and as an introduction, Economiesuisse stated that an excessive increase of VAT would be inevitable and that the BI would notably weaken the economic performance and the competitive potential of the country. Thus, it is immediately clear that the authors were even not aware of the existence of our book with the three models, published in 2010.

However, Economiesuisse had no problem with calculating the gross cost of BI per year. They assigned 25% of BI to minors in accordance with the numbers proposed since 2012 by the promoters of the initiative, and arrived at the slightly lower amount of CHF 202 bn (compared with our CHF 209 bn). Like all the other authors, they integrate the substitution of the most important parts of the current social insurance (public old age pension AHV, unemployment, child benefits, social aid, etc.), calculating a figure of CHF 62 bn, slightly under the estimates of the promoters of the popular initiative.

Up to this point, the differences are minor. From here however, the assumptions start to vary considerably. Economiesuisse works with a modelling of economic parameters, an issue not tackled here, but which is of course of interest to those dealing with the subject as such, and as well the subject of a variety of papers at different levels. The calculations within the model are based on a "simple neoclassical growth model" (Solow, Romer and others) and deliver quite negative results for the advocates of a BI. In order to cover the CHF 140 bn difference between gross cost and substitution effects, Economiesuisse foresees an increase of VAT to more than 50% (which obviously is a consequence of not taking into account any financing model other than the one proposed by Goetz Werner). According to the model, we would have the consequences of a shrinking of the GDP of 17%, and a decrease of capital stock (2011) from CHF 1,378 bn to CHF 985 bn. The latter is due to the formula applied when calculating the value of the capital stock where the tax rate plays the decisive role for the decrease.

As shown above, there are other models to be considered for a more accurate analysis of the financing question. Even the authors of the popular initiative do not speak of such a spectacular increase in VAT (or of direct taxations, otherwise), leaving the way of transferring the salary sums that would be substituted by the BI to non-specified market forces. But even within the model of Economiesuisse, there is a grave mistake. It bases the whole model on the cost side with the deficit of CHF 140 bn while the corresponding sums do not appear on the other side of the balance sheet, neither as salary substitution nor even simply as popular income. According to my numbers, CHF 110 bn should show up in the balance sheet as a kind of salary increase. If you take the compensation mechanism as a taxation on one side, you have to compensate the balance of the national economic account by a salary increase on the other, which would be the payment of the BI. Economiesuisse has forgotten to enter the detail of CHF 110 bn into its own models and equations!

The "Message" of the Federal Council

For every popular initiative that has been successfully submitted, the Federal Council establishes a "message" for the attention of parliament. Within the context of the BI popular initiative, the message is based on the numbers put forward by the promoters of the popular initiative, that is, those in the booklet of Müller and Straub – gross cost of CHF 208 bn (again with 25% of BI for minors), whereas the effect of the substitution of social security on the other side is valued at CHF 55 bn (as opposed to the CHF 70 bn of Müller and Straub). The "absorption of earned income" would be CHF 128 bn, as put forward by Müller and Straub. The absorption transfer would be done by direct taxation and would exclude the first CHF 30,000 of all earned income, and the gap would be covered by VAT (CHF 25 bn). The message mentions eventually establishing the direct tax in a progressive way, but does not enter into details.[10]

Now this kind of presentation is all but clear. It contradicts all rules, even in the case of full absorption by income tax, in that according to this mechanism, the taxpayers with the lowest incomes should pay the highest rates. Even if this assumption has only been taken for analytical purposes, it should somehow allow the chance to explore the possible mechanisms which the authors of the initiative had in mind. Obviously, it would have been preferable to see at least a serious attempt of a thorough understanding of the proposition, even if the Federal Council does not agree with it. It looks like the Federal Council does not even know exactly what it does not agree with.

Conclusion

Financing is not the core question of the BI concept. Still, certain calculations have to be done to produce some ideas about what would occur, and what would be needed if BI were to be introduced in the future. Independent from any speculation about possible effects on different parameters of the economic and social activity, the aim of this article was to establish a set of numbers that afterwards could be embellished with any desired side or main effect. It is something like the base for more speculative deliberations, like for instance about the inclination to assume, abandon, increase or reduce a salaried activity, as is and has been the subject of various scientific enquiries and papers. Our investigation has shown amongst other things, how little attention the opponents of the scheme have paid to the fundamental ideas and elements of the financing of a BI in Switzerland, which led to some miscalculations. On the other hand, the errors in the calculations of the advocates of the scheme have rather been forgiven, for they have always insisted that the most important thing is the principle, not the money: if society agrees to introduce the scheme, the specifications of the introduction will follow and will have no devastating consequences on modern life. The campaigners make the effort of doing all these somewhat strange calculations only because they have to furnish some indications, not yet grown to scientific values.

The calculations discussed within this chapter give the following results: for 2012, the gross cost of introducing BI in Switzerland is approximately CHF 209 bn per year, based on a resident population of 8 mn, of whom 1.5 mn are classed as minors under 18 years. BI would be CHF 2,500 per month per adult (at a cost of CHF 198 bn per year) and CHF 625 for minors (costing CHF 11 bn per year). Total compensation would be CHF 179 bn per year made up of CHF 111 bn from the earned income from the clearing model (or other mechanisms of transfer/absorption); CHF 63 bn from the social insurances and CHF 5 bn from other economies, for instance at the administrative level, with subsidies for the agriculture, scholarship funds, etc. that could be removed or replaced by the BI. So – contrary to the hopes I had for a short time after my initial calculations – there is a gap of some CHF 30 bn per year to fill. This is a considerable number – not as big as some opponents pretend, but far more than Müller and Straub assume. If the CHF 30 bn were borne equally by all 6.5 mn adult residents, it would be CHF 4,500 per person per year, about CHF 400 per month.

There are several possibilities to deal with this and I have discussed some technical approaches for filling the gap. The smoothest way would appear to be an increase of VAT, because somehow it hides the shocking reality of the sheer amount to pay and the increase of VAT would not translate in a linear way into price increases. In practice, parliament would probably choose some mixed method of financing. An increase of VAT by 5% would cover half the cost, reducing the average contribution of income tax per year shown in Table 3.6 by 50%.

This would be affordable, but still a considerable amount – corresponding to a tax hike of about 5% of the earned income, leading to an increase of the tax rate of 20% and more – and it is more than questionable if this is politically feasible. Voters anyway and above all need to understand what changes they would pay for, otherwise the proposal would never succeed in a popular vote and in parliament. They have to see that this is not a financial raid by the poor on the purse of the middle class (which is currently the mainstream political discussion in Switzerland), but the introduction of a basic new and fair way of managing society which requires a long overdue adjustment to both legal and actual living conditions. The main beneficiaries would not be the poor and/or the lazy, but primarily couples with children.

Just one remark about this last point. According to practice and ideology, the labour market in our modern society is what it is. It has never been questioned that the same salary for the same work should, in one case, be enough to satisfy the needs of a family of say two adults and two children and in another case of one single person. (The compensatory factors of tax allowances and child allowances do not really make a significant difference, at least not in Switzerland.) This is funny, in a certain way, and shows how the public opinion accepts the most evident inequalities, if not injustices without blinking an eye, just because it is what it is. The introduction of BI puts an end to this obvious and basic injustice without even changing a comma in how the labour market functions. I am convinced that voters are ready to pay something for improvements to modernise our society and the BI is going to become one of the important institutions of this modern society. But I am not sure if they are ready to pay the entire bill as presented here. There are other options to be considered.

The most interesting option to me seems to be the evaluation of the financial possibilities arising from the end of the capital-building period of the second pillar of the old age insurance.[11] The potential saving of CHF 10 to 20 bn per year could reduce the gap (and thus all the working hypotheses mentioned above) by half, starting from the year 2025. To be fair, I admit that the politicians dealing with pension plans have probably already reserved these funds to cover deficits arising from the demographic evolution with the increasing share of the old age population. But since the BI covers the basic payments of the mandatory state old age pension (AHV) in the first place, this could work out even within this kind of endeavour.

The introduction of a BI has got to be conceived as a process. Once the initiative is approved by the people, parliament could consider different options to minimise the cost. For example by starting with a slightly lower level of BI than we have used above (a BI of around CHF 2,000 per month per adult and CHF 625 per month per minor would be cost neutral), meaning that some parts of the social security system would need to be maintained for longer, or the BI for retired people would need to be higher to equal the level of the former AHV or complementary benefits would need to increase. Another option could be a gradual introduction of a BI, for instance starting with a BI for children (see for instance the contribution of Ingmar Kumpmann and Ingrid Hohenleitner in our book; BIEN-Suisse, Jörimann and Kündig 2010) apart from the coverage of those who are retired.

When it comes to a macroeconomic view of the introduction of a fully fledged BI, we state that the financing of the CHF 30 bn gap would not take funds from national consumer spending (which rather, is strengthened by BI because it tends to give more to those with less spending power); it would finance the gap from the savings pot. And here we come back to some basic questions in the context of savings and finance. Goetz Werner commented at the BI Congress in Munich 2012 on savings as one of the reasons for the global financial crises. For him, there were indications that from time to time, massive levels of savings appeared to be the enemy of the real economy – the economic apparatus that guaranteed our daily lives – because corporate savings, as well private savings of the wealthy and also of the middle class, for instance within the mandatory professional old age savings plans, were directed less into productive investments and increasingly into capital markets, which at a given point could collapse because of savings overload, amongst other reasons. This meant that from time to time, our attempts to prepare for the future were damaging (maybe even structurally and inherently) our present lives. There are many discussions about the continuous dislocation from earned income towards capital revenue, etc. In this sense it is quite superficial to say that the middle classes are always bound to finance the poor – the problem is a different one.

Finally, I should like to quote a macroeconomic reflection that in a way, illustrates the dimension of the venture. Martino Rossi et al. (1995)[12] and others say that the BI ought to be considered as a third, constitutive element of modern national economies. Up to now, its harvest has been divided between capital and wages, and in the future, it should be divided into three parts – capital, wages and BI.

Notes

1. SKOS, Guidances, http://skos.ch/skos-richtlinien/.
2. For the "Latte-Macchiato-These" see http://www.grundeinkommen.ch/milchschaum/.
3. Das Solidarische Bürgergeld, see http://www.dieter-althaus.de.
4. Figures are from Financial statistics of Switzerland 2012 (for the year 2010), annual report, Federal Finance Department.
5. For the full text of the initiative, see https://www.admin.ch/ch/d/pore/vi/vis423t.html.
6. http://zukunft.ch/potentialanalyse-grundeinkommen.pdf.

7. Gerfin/Leu, Die Volkswirtschaft Nr. 6/2005; Schaltegger, Fed. Tax Administration, 2004.
8. Tobias Müller, Partizipationseinkommen: ein wirkungsvolles Instrument im Kampf gegen die Armut? Die Volkswirtschaft 7/2004, aktualisiert in Soziale Sicherheit 4/2008, BSV, Bern.
9. http://www.economiesuisse.ch/sites/default/files/downloads/dp21_grundeinkommen_print.pdf.
10. Full text of the "message": https://www.admin.ch/opc/de/federal-gazette/2014/6551.pdf.
11. Otherwise, up to now none of the BI promoters has considered using any funds of the second pillar for the financing of the BI in Switzerland, although this semiprivate professional old age pension scheme (mandatory for salaries above 20,000 CHF/year) has got some weaknesses, above all at the lower end of the earned income scale. Obviously, this part of the old age insurance does not exist at all for persons who have not been able to exercise any professional activity.
12. Martino Rossi, economist, researcher, former municipal counsellor of Lugano.

REFERENCES

Althaus, D. et al.: Das Solidarische Bürgergeld [German], http://www.dieteralthaus.de.
BIEN Suisse, [ed.]. (2010) Le financement d'un revenu de base [French]. Zurich: Seismo.
Economiesuisse. (October 2012) Paper on the Basic Income Initiative: http://www.economiesuisse.ch/sites/default/files/downloads/dp21_grundeinkommen_print.pdf.
Gerfin, M./Leu, R.E. Die Volkswirtschaft Nr. 6/2005.
Initiative Grundeinkommen; for the "Latte-Macchiato-These": http://www.grundeinkommen.ch/milchschaum/.
Initiative Grundeinkommen; full text of the initiative: https://www.admin.ch/ch/d/pore/vi/vis423t.html.
Müller, T. Partizipationseinkommen: ein wirkungsvolles Instrument im Kampf gegen die Armut? Die Volkswirtschaft 7/2004, aktualisiert in Soziale Sicherheit 4/2008. Bern: BSV.
Rossi, M. et al. (1995) Ripensare la Solidarietà [Italian]. Locarno: Dadò.
Schaltegger, C. A. (2004) Die negative Einkommenssteuer, Reformoption für die Schweiz? [German], 2004 Swiss Federal Tax Administration.
Schweiz. Konferenz für Sozialhilfe (Swiss Conference of Social Assistance) SKOS, Guidances, http://skos.ch/skos-richtlinien/ [German].

Straub, D., and C. Müller. (2012) *Die Befreiung der Schweiz (The Rescue of Switzerland)* [German]. Zurich: Limmat Verlag.
Swiss Federal Council; full text of the "message" of the Federal Council: https://www.admin.ch/opc/de/federal-gazette/2014/6551.pdf.
Swiss Federal Social Insurance Office: Pocket statistics of the Social Insurances in Switzerland 2014.
Swiss Federal Statistical Office, various statistics.
Van Parijs, P. (1995) *Real Freedom For All*. Oxford: Clerendon Press.
Werner, G. W. (2007) *Einkommen für alle* [German]. Köln: Kiepenheuer und Witsch.

Albert Jörimann *1955, until 2013 president of BIEN-Switzerland, since then independent researcher; lives in Zurich, Switzerland.

PART 3

Building Up BIG

CHAPTER 4

Total Economic Rents of Australia as a Source for Basic Income

Gary Flomenhoft

Abstract Interest in basic income (BI) has resurged from the realization that artificial intelligence (AI) is replacing human beings in the workforce. Therefore, it is urgent to resolve the controversial question of how to finance BI, overcoming objections to presumed violations of property rights. This chapter argues that resources produced by nature or society as a whole, are the property of the public. Therefore the citizenry are entitled to receive rent for use of their property, what economists call economic rent. Figures from the *Total Resource Rents of Australia (TRRA)* study is used to calculate revenue available for BI in Australia.

Keywords Economic rent · Basic income · Land rent · Dividend · Royalties · Commons and common assets

Basic income (BI), or guaranteed annual income as it was referred to in the past, is once again on the policy agenda worldwide. This is partly due to the tireless efforts of advocates who have been researching and promoting

---

G. Flomenhoft (✉)
Gund Institute for Ecological Economics, University of Vermont, Burlington, VT, USA

Centre for Social Responsibility in Mining, Sustainable Minerals Institute (SMI), University of Queensland, Brisbane, Australia

© The Author(s) 2017
R. Pereira (ed.), *Financing Basic Income*, Exploring the Basic Income Guarantee, DOI 10.1007/978-3-319-54268-3_4

it through periods of great interest like the McGovern/Nixon era in the US, when both major political parties advocated the idea, through periods of low interest during the recent neoliberal era. Stalwarts continued their work such as with the creation of the BI Earth Network (BIEN) organization in Europe and the BI Group (BIG) organization in the US. One noteworthy person is the late Al Sheahan, who wrote and worked on BI tirelessly from the late 1960s until his death in 2013, to whom I dedicate this chapter.

Recently, interest has revived due to one issue in particular. Policy analysts have suddenly realized that automation and artificial intelligence (AI) are putting people out of work, and economic growth is slowing down. A typical news report online states that robots will replace 50% of human jobs in next 10–20 years.[1] Some robots in Japan are already serving as hotel desk clerks and receptionists. This has jolted people into serious consideration of how to finance people when they no longer have jobs. The lacklustre recovery from the Global Financial Crisis (GFC), and growing inequality has also motivated renewed consideration of BI.

John Stuart Mill in his conception of the "stationary state" early imagined the leisure society, which was also expected by John Maynard Keynes in his projections of the future, both expecting machinery to replace human labour to a very significant extent. The problem then as now was how would people get paid.

One of the most contentious issues has always been the question of how to finance a guaranteed income. The main objection is the common aversion to giving people "something for nothing", and the redistribution of income that would result from most tax-based schemes that are commonly discussed in Europe. The longest lasting, currently operating BI scheme is the Alaska Permanent Fund Dividend,[2] which provides between US$1,000 and $2,000 per year to every resident of Alaska over the age of one. This plan avoids the thorny issue of income redistribution altogether, by basing the dividend checks on royalties from oil on state land, what economists call economic rent. A pair of recent books on the Alaska system explore this model (Widerquist and Howard 2012a, b).

Economic rent is defined as the unearned income from production of a good after all expenses are paid, including a normal rate of profit. Sometimes it is called "windfall" profit, but it comes from payment for a production factor that has no production cost. Oil in the ground was produced by nature at no cost. It was created by geological processes over millions of years. Human beings had nothing to do with its creation. Although prospecting, exploration, well drilling, extraction, refining, transporting, etc.

all have costs, the price of oil normally far exceeds these costs including a normal rate of profit. This is the source of unearned economic rent. Figure 4.1 shows the cost of extraction of oil from various countries around the world. When oil hit $147 per barrel in 2007, the economic rent (shaded portion above cost figures) ranged from $57 to $125 per barrel depending on the cost of extraction. Oil prices have recently dropped very low, which makes many wells uneconomical, but there is still economic rent from many wells.

Economic rent derives from the social and natural commons that are created by nature or by society as a whole.[3] If it comes from the commons, then by definition it is public not private property. Therefore, no one's income is taken when rent is collected, so there is no redistribution, the bogeyman of many conservatives. There are two opposing theories of economic rent, the democratic theory and the liberal theory. John Warnock describes them this way:

> The democratic theory of rent suggests that governments should maximize their collection of rent to the benefit of their publics, who own the resources. The liberal theory of rent suggests that public resources should be privatized and employed to make profits, and that rents should remain in private hands either entirely, or enough to ensure investment in the industry. (Warnock 2006: 6)

One approach to BI is to base it on the democratic theory of rent, with the assumption that the commons belongs to the public. John Locke and Thomas Paine's theories of property both supported this contention. Locke said that the commons belongs to all and the only justification for private land is if there is "as much and as good left in common for others". Locke contended that private property arises from the application of labour to the commons (Locke 1698). Likewise, Paine believed that the Earth is the common property of humanity, and it is only the products of labour that are private (Paine 1797). There is ample justification for the commons belonging to the public. This principle can be expanded to many natural resources besides oil, and extended to socially produced resources as well.

It is on this basis that Karl Fitzgerald updated the figures of the late Tony O'Brien's *Total Resource Rents of Australia (TRRA)* (1999) in 2013. Fitzgerald's report is based on the following categories of economic rent: Land Rent, Natural Monopolies, and Resource Rents, then adds in Sin Taxes and Non-Tax Receipts. The total figure amounts to AU$386.9 billion annually, which compares favourably to total government operating revenue at all levels of $390.1 billion. For economic rent alone, the total is

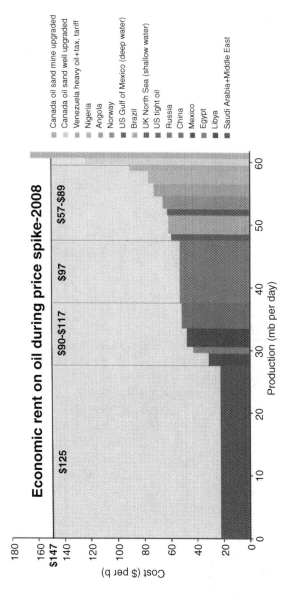

Fig. 4.1 Economic rent from oil extraction

$340.7 billion. With a 2016 Australia population of 24,050,120 this economic rent amounts to $14,166 per person.

For this exercise we will assume that taxes are retained in order to fund all existing government programs and services, so we must subtract existing revenue from estimated economic rent to see what remains. We do not want to shortchange government of existing revenues, so we will subtract these from our total and only count additional economic rent generated. This does not account for the change in tax revenues that results from the collection of economic rent, or the payment of a BI. That is beyond the scope of this article, but would be worth pursuing in further research. There are several aspects to these dynamic changes that would need to be accounted for as explained in the following paragraphs.

The primary argument of conservatives and libertarians who favour guaranteed income going back to Milton Friedman, and more recently Charles A. Murray, is the huge reduction in bureaucracy and means testing infrastructure that would result, and thus the expected reduction of government expenditures. They also make moral claims on incentives and motivation, which we will leave aside. For the US, on strictly financial terms Murray claims, "This statement does not take transition costs into account, a complex issue that I set aside here except to note that a system that costs a trillion dollars less per year than the current system by 2028" (Murray 2008: 4). Murray also lists many knock-on effects such as reduced crime, reduced unwanted births, less elderly poverty, better health, etc. We are unable to account for these effects here.

Tony O'Brien listed the following savings in his *1999 Total Resource Rents of Australia* report (Fitzgerald 2013: 42):

Potential savings from the introduction of a Site and Resource Rent system and the removal of all other taxes could be extremely large, approaching one third of total current government outlays.

Many of the following expenses would be greatly reduced or in some cases eliminated:

- the cost of assessing, collecting and endeavouring to prevent the evasion of existing taxes
- the cost of relieving involuntary unemployment and poverty which will decline and disappear as employment revives
- the use by governments of tax concession and other privileges as "sweeteners" to solicit or hold large corporations
- the cost of land acquisition for public purposes

Fitzgerald also cites savings in the pharmaceutical and the welfare budgets.

The second major financial impact results from the collection of economic rent on residential land. Although it is counter-intuitive to most people, the collection of a 5–6% land rent or land tax per year eliminates much of the unearned income from owning real estate, therefore reduces capital gains and speculation, and thus reduces its demand and should reduce its price. For homeowners, given a fixed average income level, if a larger share of income is spent on land taxes, this reduces the remaining amount of income left to pay for mortgages, providing a further impetus for reduced prices. It essentially substitutes a tax payment for mortgage payment. There is ample mathematical proof of this in the literature, so we won't delve into it here. The point is that the collection of economic rent on land could reduce the price of housing, which could improve disposable income, and therefore the need for housing subsidies and other transfer payments. There are a total of $71 billion in annual housing subsidies in Australia due to the inflated value of land, the largest being the capital gains tax exemption ($45 billion), and land tax exemption for owner-occupied property ($9.5 billion) (Flomenhoft 2016).

The third financial impact resulting from collection of economic rent is the reduction of so-called deadweight losses in production. This is due to paying for things that have no production cost, and allowing this revenue to accumulate in private hands instead of the public, according to the liberal theory of rent. We will not account for these benefits either.

On the progressive side of the spectrum many moral and ethical arguments have been made based on the prerogative of reducing poverty due to compassion and solidarity with the less fortunate, and also in favour of greater freedom (Van Parijs 1998). We will leave these arguments aside for now as well.

A BI using economic rent avoids all these practical and ethical arguments completely, especially the thorny issue of income redistribution, which is a major stumbling block to adoption of BI. The democratic theory of rent simply says that people are entitled to these payments because it is their property. No one disputes that a person owning stocks is entitled to dividends, that an apartment owner is entitled to collection of rent from tenants or that an owner of an oil well is entitled to royalties. Conservative Alaskans conceive of oil on state land as their property, and therefore support receiving a dividend check from Permanent Fund revenue. We won't address the question of the possible work disincentive, because wealthy trust-fund beneficiaries, and people living from investments still seem to find productive uses of their time, whether for work or philanthropy. It is only the poor who apparently will become lazy if given unearned income. But we won't debate this.

The confusion arises when states assume the right to dispose of common property on behalf of the people. In more capitalistic countries, governments often grant ownership of the commons to the private sector in a process of privatization and sell-off of state assets. In more socialist leaning or even many capitalistic states (such as Alaska) governments may retain ownership of common assets, and use revenue for governmental services and infrastructure. Whether the people benefit or not depends on the level of democracy. We could compare use of oil revenue in democratic Norway, which has a nearly $1 trillion dollar oil fund, to a dictatorship like Saudi Arabia, where the commons are simply the property of the ruling family and the country is basically a private oil corporation. The state is not the equivalent of the public, and payment of BI from economic rent recognizes the commons as public property, not the property of the state, feudal lords or sheiks. Alaska uses oil revenues for both state funding and for the Permanent Fund and Dividend, so has elements of state and public ownership of oil rent.

The key point of Fitzgerald's *Total Resource Rents of Australia* (TRRA), is that there are many other sources of economic rent besides oil and minerals. Flomenhoft has documented 12 different common assets that could generate $10,348 of economic rent per person per year in the resource-poor state of Vermont, USA (Widerquist and Howard 2012b: 105). Natural assets in Vermont tabulated include fisheries and wildlife, public forests, ground and surface water, minerals, wind for wind power, and the atmosphere as a sink for CO_2 and other emissions. Socially created common assets included were the Internet and World Wide Web, the electromagnetic (EM) broadcast spectrum, the financial and monetary systems and the value of all land.

Fitzgerald has done a more extensive job identifying approximately 20 different sources of economic rent in Australia in Table 4.1 (Fitzgerald 2013: 5).

Fitzgerald divides the revenue into the following categories:

Part II - Calculation of economic rent
Part III – Natural monopolies
Part IV – The frontiers of monopoly
Part V – Existing government revenue

We will explore them to understand how these calculations were made.

Table 4.1 Total resource rents of Australia

Item	Valuation $million	% of valuation	Raised $million
Land – residential	2,794,800	5.5%	153,714
Land – commercial	338,500	6.5%	22,002
Land – rural	263,700	5.5%	14,504
Land – other	287,700	5.5%	15,791
Subsoil minerals	$(67,359+14.637)^1$	40%	32,813
Oil and gas – PRR	20,229	40%	8,092
Water rights	50,000	2.60%	1,300
Taxi licenses	25,000	$14,402^2$	360
Airports	1,919	40%	765
Utilities	220,000	10%	22,000
Fishing licenses	2,100	40%	840
Forestry	1800	2.7%	50
Gambling license	18,450	40%	7,380
EM spectrum	10,560	20%	2,122
Satellite orbit rights	5,100	10%	510
Internet infrastructure	64,500	10%	6,450
Domain name registration	100	3 million^3	300
Banking license fees	43,427	40%	17,371
Corporate commons fee	1,382,000	2%	27,640
Patents	12,980	0.005%	65
Parking fees	Estimate		250
Public transport	Estimate		2,400
Liquor licenses	Govt budget		4,000
Vehicle rego, driver license	Govt budget		5,294
Sin taxes – tobacco, alcohol	Govt budget		12,510
Carbon tax	$(4,020 +14,200)^4$		18,220
Govt non-tax receipts	20,323	50%	10,162
Total			**386,905**

^{1}40% of BHP, RIO, and Xstrata EBITDAX (2011–2012) + shareholder dividends
^{2}Number of taxi licenses 14,402 × $25,000 each = $360 million
^{3}$100/domain × 3 million domains = $300 million
^{4}Increase in petrol and diesel excise taxes during carbon tax regime

Land Rent

Land is the largest asset in any economy and rent from land constitutes 52.8% of the total rent calculation in this report (Fitzgerald 2013:19). Fitzgerald used a figure of 5.5% for residential, rural and other land, and 6.5% for commercial land. Residential land comprises 75% of the total land value in Australia. The land rent percentage was chosen as "just below long term growth trends". The annual increase in land value that is typical of real estate bubbles worldwide can be seen as land rent capitalized into the price of land. When it is not collected it accrues to owners. Polanyi pointed out in 1944 that land, along with money and labour, is a fictitious commodity, that results in devastating effects on society when it is sold in markets (Polanyi 1944). The long-term trend of land prices is somewhat higher than 5.5–6.5% in Australia. From June 2014 to June 2015, land value increased from $4197.3 billion to $4722.2 billion for an increase of $524.9 billion, or 12.5%.[4] According to the HSBC, Australian home prices have risen to 24% in the past 3 years, with Sydney jumping by 39%.[5] The long-term trend is shown in Fig. 4.2. Total Australian land values increased from $665.1 billion in 1989 to $4267.5 billion in 2014 for a total increase of 541.6%. On an annual basis over 25 years this amounts to a long-term trend of 7.72% increase per year for all land.

Fitzgerald calculates potential land rent of $206.01 billion on a total land value of $3.684 trillion using the 5.5–6.5% rate. Existing land taxes are estimated at 2.5% giving existing revenue of $91.1 billion. Subtracting existing revenue from estimated land rent leaves a total of $113.9 billion in annual land rent available for BI. This comprises the largest portion of total economic rent out of a total of $252.5 billion or 45% of total rent.

Resource Rents

The TRRA report proposes a reformed Mineral Resource Rent Tax (MRRT) to base revenues on a 40% charge on Earnings Before Interest, Tax, Depreciation, Amortization and Exploration (EBITDAX). This is justified by countries such as Norway which have a 60% state ownership of oil production,[6] plus an ordinary corporate tax of 25%, 53% special tax rate and 78% marginal tax rate on profits.[7] The findings were calculated on the EBITDAX (2011–2012) earnings of the big three mining companies – BHP Billiton, Rio Tinto, and Xstrata – totalling $67.359 billion. An additional $14.637 billion was added to EBITDAX totals to incorporate shareholder dividends paid. At a 40% rate, this sees a contribution from the entire mining sector of $32.8 billion. By comparison, in 2011–2012 the Australian government expected to earn just $1.5 billion from the mining and petroleum sector. Shareholders received $14.6 billion from the big three mining companies over this same period.

In the petroleum and gas sector, according to the Australia Bureau of Statistics (ABS), the oil and gas extractions industry EBITDAX was

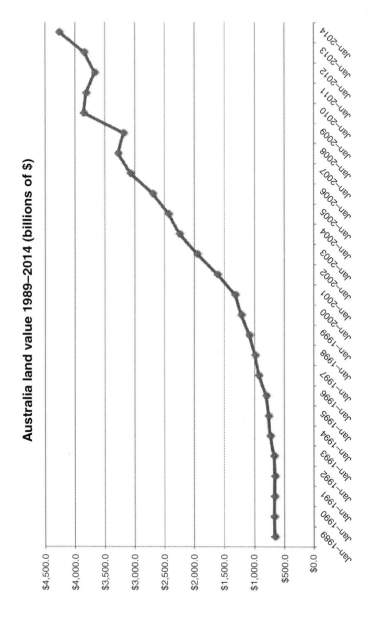

Fig. 4.2 Total Australian land prices 1989–2014 (**Note:** Australian Bureau of Statistics (ABS) 5204.0 – Australian System of National Accounts, 2014–2015, Table 61, column AT: http://www.abs.gov.au/AUSSTATS/abs@.nsf/DetailsPage/5204.02014–15?OpenDocument)

calculated at $22.229 billion (2010–11). A 40% resource rent was levied to calculate the $8.092 billion contribution to government revenue. Adding minerals and petroleum product revenue together totals $40.9 billion. Subtracting $1.5 billion from existing revenue leaves $39.4 billion for BI.

EM Spectrum

Television licenses were given away in the 1950s according to Fitzgerald. Recently Australia auctioned portions of the 700 MHz EM spectrum. The sale raised $1.96 billion in one-off revenue for the 15-year license. This is equivalent to $133 million per year in payment. More than $1 billion of spectrum remains unsold. The ABS calculates the existing spectrum already allocated at $8.6 billion. If we add the recent $1.96 billion auction, the total is $10.56 billion. A 20% resource rent on the $10.56 billion total will see the multimedia industry (radio, TV, mobile) contribute $2.12 billion per annum. Subtracting $133 million from $2.12 billion per year leaves $1.989 billion for BI. This may be significantly undervalued as total spectrum value in the US is estimated at $1 trillion, according to the US economist J.H Snider (2003).

Corporate Commons

Peter Barnes relates an experience when he considered taking "Working Assets" the phone company he started public. "Our investment banker informed us that, simply by going public, we'd increase the value of our stock by 30%. He called this magic a liquidity premium. What he meant was that stock that can be sold in a market of millions is worth more than stock that has almost no market at all. This extra value would come not from anything we did, but from the socially created bonus of liquidity. We'd be reaping what others sowed" (Barnes 2006). The SEC, the stock exchanges and all the other social institutions that allowed the stock market to function, created a premium of 30% in public companies. Fitzgerald calculated a 2% corporate commons fee on the 2013 Australia Stock Exchange market capitalization of $1.382 trillion delivering $27.64 billion in annual revenue. If 30% of the value of public companies is due to the existence of the stock market itself, then 2% is rather modest. Barnes calls it liquidity rent.

WATER

According to Fitzgerald, Water Entitlement holders currently pay no resource rents, and the ABS does not value the licenses in the national accounts. Robert O'Brien, managing director of Percat Water, writes that there are 140,000 license holders, with an estimated value of the water market of $50 billion.[8] Additionally, the value of access to underground aquifers has not been included. In Vermont and other US states groundwater, like surface water, has been declared a public trust resource. If government holds water in trust for the public, then government is also entitled to collect rent on behalf of the public who are its owners. With the value of 2012 Water Entitlements holding up despite regular rainfall, the report includes a 2.6% resource rent on this monopoly right. Applying that rate to O'Brien's $50 billion valuation results in an estimated $1.3 billion contribution to economic rent.

PUBLIC UTILITY PRIVATIZATION

In the TRRA report it is stated that in October 2012, Infrastructure Australia (IA) spearheaded a move to privatize $220 billion in public assets via the sale of 82 government entities. Three existing public utilities pay a dividend of $3.2 billion to NSW, QLD, and VIC government. 79 others do not. The $220 billion valuation does not include existing private utilities. The utilities are natural monopolies, and privatization often results in higher prices. According to Queensland Energy Minister Stephen Robertson, public utilities in Queensland have lower prices than private utilities in Victoria.[9] Privatization of electrical utilities resulted in the collapse of Enron in the US, after Enron manipulated electric rates in California and bankrupted several private utilities. Public utilities did not suffer the same fate. Enron traders were recorded complaining about having to pay back all the money they stole from price gouging "those poor grandmothers in California".[10]

Fitzgerald calculates monopoly rents attributable to utilities in water, power, ports, rail and non-privatized airports at 10% on the $220 billion in assets for a total of $22 billion.

AIRPORTS

According to Fitzgerald, Australia and the UK are the only two nations in the world to have privatized their airports. To prove that this results in monopoly rent, Clive Domain has written, "Sydney Airport made an operating profit of $773 million on $943 million in revenue. That's an operating margin of 82 per cent; the airport had to spend only $170 million to make nearly a billion. Through the miracle of accounting, Sydney airport last year lost $131 million after allowances for depreciation, debt servicing and other devices it is able to use".[11]

If government grants a monopoly to private business then it has the right to charge rent for the privilege. The TRRA report set the monopoly charge at 40% of EBITDA, amounting to $765 million in revenue.

Taxi Licenses

Government restricts the supply of taxi licenses, which creates scarcity rent. Although license holders only pay $512 per year for the privilege, 70% of licenses are leased to operators for around $30,000 per year. The average sale price of a license from 2003–2011 was over $400,000 in Brisbane and Melbourne. A Victorian Taxi Industry Inquiry suggested raising the annual fee to $25,000 to recapture the monopoly rent from license holders. The TRRA report adopts this recommendation and calculates potential revenue of $360,050,000 from a total of 14,402 licenses in Australia at $25,000 apiece. This formula may have to be changed as the paradigm of paid passenger travel is being severely challenged by Uber, Lyft and other ride services. The monopoly is being broken, which may significantly lower the value of a taxi license. This may just mean transferring the rental fee to a larger number of private vehicle operators.

Fishing Licenses and Quotas

Many valuable fishing licenses and quotas were given out for free but are now sold for large amounts of money. Fitzgerald cites bluefin tuna, abalone, jellyfish and the Northern Prawn Fishery, as fisheries generating large rents for license owners. He points out that "tuna king" Tony Santic sold Bluefin tuna quotas for $214,000 per tonne in the 1990s, to justify collection of rent on this government giveaway. Existing revenue from levy fees is given as $13.8 million on an industry valued in 2009–2010 at $2.18 billion. The report uses a 40% resource rent on $2.18 billion to generate $840 million of potential economic rent.

Forestry

The "commercial in confidence" nature of Australia's privatized forests makes data hard to come by. The same problem was encountered in the Vermont study. Information is proprietary. Nevertheless some information was available. According to the TRRA report, the Department of Agriculture, Fisheries and Forestry (DAFF) collects just five cents per cubic metre of timber and only 3.5 cents per cubic metre for export hardwood woodchip. In 2010–2011, Australia's production forests had a gross value of around $1.84 billion. DAFF collected $1.325 million for timber harvested equating to a royalty payment of 0.007%. This royalty does not come close to covering road subsidies and direct government contributions to the industry. The report estimates $50 million of potential revenue based on the annual production of $1.8 billion at a royalty of 2.7%. Fitzgerald (2013: 36) claims, "In years to come these forests will earn carbon credits and significantly increase in value according to their carbon sequestering capacity. The battle over who earns these carbon credits will be a hot issue".

Gambling

According to the TRRA report, 198,725 poker machines operate nationwide, delivering a net gambling surplus of $18.45 billion (2009–2010). The Victoria government has identified at least $50,000 per poker machine as economic rent, since the rights are auctioned for $5,500 and the machine makes $80,000 per year. $50,000 out of $80,000 is 62.5% economic rent. The TRRA report therefore makes a modest recommendation of 40% rent on the gambling surplus. A 40% resource rent on the $18.45 billion surplus would deliver $7.38 billion per year. (This is a correction on the report figure of $7.6 billion.) Deducting existing gambling revenues of $5.1 billion (2010–2011) from $7.38 billion, leaves a balance for BI of $2.28 billion. (Fitzgerald 2013: 36, 37).

Privatized Public Transport Providers

When public transit systems are built, land around transit stops increases greatly in value. Some municipalities recapture this value through special assessments in order to finance the transit system through the value they create. This is referred to as "value capture" or "value recapture". The

Melbourne Transit Rail operates the Melbourne train network and is also granted development rights above the train stations. The eight major city public transport systems are calculated to contribute $2.4 billion in revenue. Existing revenue consists of Sydney's RailCorp $74 million in payroll taxes and fringe benefits in 2010–2011, which must be subtracted.

Cybersquatting of Internet Domain Names

The term "cybersquatting" refers to purchasing a domain name, which a related business will one day see value in. For example, domains such as sextoys.com.au sold for $20,000, fridges.com.au for $25,500 and invest mentproperty.com.au for $125,000. It was reported that Apple paid at least US$1 million to Michael Kovatch for the transfer of the iPhone.com domain name. No economic value is added by the middleman acquiring the domain for a registration price of as little as A$1. Any selling price above this is a pure economic rent. According to Deloitte Access Economics, by August 2012 total domain names registered in Australia reached over 3 million. The TRRA report recommends a fee of $100 to collect this monopoly rent and to discourage holding domain names out of use for future unearned profit. Applied to 3 million domain names, this will result in $300 million revenue.

Patents

Patents are a government-granted monopoly for a fixed period of time on research and development (R&D) investments. According to the Australian Bureau of Statistics (ABS), the mean lifespans of standard patents filed in Australia between 1980 and 2001 were between 10 and 13 years.[12]

The example of "patents on life" can be used to explain the logic of collecting a share of patent value. The patenting of genome sequences such as the BRAC1 and BRAC2 cancer genes is very controversial. Prime Minister Turnbull is quoted as stating that, "Companies holding these patents are able to charge very high fees to anyone who wants to test to see if the gene exists within their own bodies". If a patent is a government-granted monopoly, it is reasonable for the government to recover some of this cost from patent holders.

The ABS accounted for R&D spending in 2007–2008 with an increase in Gross Capital Formation of AU$320 billion, and estimated GDP increase of $12.9 billion. Fitzgerald uses the R&D impact on GDP as a proxy for patents, and proposes a minimal 0.005% charge on 2007–2008 ABS R&D value of $12.98 billion, providing revenue of $64.9 million. Further analysis can more accurately determine the value of the monopoly privilege granted to patent holders, while maintaining the incentive to invent.

SATELLITE ORBITS

The collection of rent on satellite orbits above Australian airspace is a questionable assertion in light of current space law. Carol Buxton points out that satellite orbital slots are allocated according to the *a priori*, or the *posteriori* system which means "first in time, first in right" (Buxton 2004: 689). The International Telecommunications Union (ITU) has granted some orbital slots as the need arises, favoured by the countries having space technology. "The a *priori* system, however, allots a number of slots to each nation, regardless of whether use of the slots will ever occur. Because less-developed nations fear that they will lose access to orbital slots due to their insufficient technology, they prefer the latter [a priori] system" (Buxton 2004: 703). The drawback of the *a priori* system was demonstrated by Tonga, which applied for 16 orbital slots, and was eventually granted six. Tonga then auctioned five allotments for $2 million per year for each orbit, and leased the remaining allotment. This demonstrates the problem with granting property rights to agents who do not plan to use the resource, but can profit from the labour of others, a form of exploitation.

> In 1976, several less-developed nations located at the equator claimed territorial sovereignty over the geo-stationary orbit with the Bogota Declaration. The nations contended that the natural resources of each sovereignty necessarily included the geostationary orbit above that territory. Though the Declaration directly conflicted with the Outer Space Treaty, which prohibits national appropriation of space, it became "effective as a political device that brought attention to developing countries" concerns over being prohibited access to the geo-stationary orbit by developed countries that already possessed the technological skills and resources necessary to utilize the resource'. This resulted in the implementation of Article 33 of the ITU's Radio

Regulations, which requires that the ITU consider "the special needs of developing countries and the geographical situation of particular countries". The entire system directly conflicts with the Outer Space Treaty if the ITU grants slots to nations because the Outer Space Treaty expressly prohibits national appropriation. The ITU seems to focus on the idea of "access" rather than ownership. (Buxton 2004: 705)

The Space Foundation estimated the global satellite industry generated $257 billion in 2008. The TRRA report uses the Australian 2% share of global GDP applied to the satellite industry's $257 billion to get a figure of $5.1 billion. A 10% resource rent would generate a $510 million contribution. This figure might be considerably higher now due to the growth in data traffic since the calculation of these 2009 figures. Rather than basing rent on usage of airspace over Australia, the allocation of orbital slots by the ITU is bound to generate some rents. Since their slots are scarce, any Australian company which is able to acquire an orbital slot, is likely to have access to a partial monopoly, which generates rents. This scarcity rent might be a better source for the orbital rent.

Internet Infrastructure

The Internet itself was created by taxpayer funding in the US through the military research arm Defense Advanced Research Projects Agency (DARPA). Internet service providers (ISPs) charge users for access to the Internet. Therefore, it is not unreasonable for the public to consider charging ISPs for access to the publicly created Internet. If a private company had developed the Internet, but other companies were using it and charging people for access, I am sure that company would be suing for its property rights. But the public has no such advocate for the right to its property. Government is typically dominated by economic interests who favour the liberal theory of rent, giving them ownership rights to the commons.

According to the TRRA report, the cost of installing Australia's National Broadband Network (NBN) is expected to be $43 billion with existing Internet infrastructure estimated at half that value. Since this is a public investment, surely Internet service providers should not be granted ongoing use of it for free since they charge users for access. Fitzgerald proposes a 10% resource rent on the $64.5 billion existing asset base providing $6.45 billion in revenue annually from the industry, including NBN and Internet service providers such as Bigpond, Optus and iiNet. Sir Tim Berners Lee created the World Wide Web including URL, http and html protocols in his spare time working at the *Conseil Européen pour la Recherche Nucléaire* (CERN) in Geneva, but required CERN to provide it as an open source common to everyone, so it would not be appropriate to charge for access.

Banking Licenses

The publicly granted privilege of banks to create money through bank loans may be the most valuable public asset given away by government. According to the Bank of England private banks create 97% of the money supply through loans,[13] of which 75–80% are mortgage loans. Professor Michael Hudson has stated, "a property is worth whatever a bank will lend, because that is the price that new buyers will be able to pay for it".[14] Reforms to land rent proposed in the report would curtail banks' ability to profit from capitalized land rents. Since property makes up a major proportion of their balance sheets, a reduction in property prices will affect their capital base. Another approach is to enforce 100% reserve requirements on banks, which would prevent them from creating credit and would restrict them to only loaning out deposits on hand, serving as intermediaries between depositors (savers) and borrowers. If there is any doubt that banks create money, consider that private central banks in the US, EU and Japan have created trillions of dollars in "quantitative easing" a euphemism for (electronic) money printing. This money was then given to banks in exchange for their non-performing assets.

Profits for the big four Australian banks (National Australia Bank [NAB], Commonwealth Bank [CBA], Australia and New Zealand Banking Group [ANZ] and Westpac [WBC]) totalled $27 billion (cash basis, 2011–2012), with dividends of $16 billion. A 40% resource rent is proposed on these earnings, which delivers $17.317 billion in rent for the value of a banking license. Revenue would increase with the inclusion of the rest of the banking industry (Fitzgerald 2013: 41).

Carbon Taxes

At the time the TRRA report was written the carbon tax was in effect. It has since been repealed. It is listed as existing government revenue, but is really rent for use of the atmosphere as a sink for waste. In the past the impact of Carbon dioxide (CO_2) on the climate was unknown, but it is now obvious that the climate is changing due to anthropogenic greenhouse gases including carbon dioxide (CO_2), nitrous oxide (N_2O) and methane (CH_4). Charging rent for use of the atmosphere as a dump for waste helps to reduce emissions, due to increasing the price of fossil fuels, and can also provide revenue to mitigate the impacts.

2011–2012 carbon taxes increased from $4 billion to $18.2 billion by moving the petrol and diesel excise taxes to the source, meeting efficiency outcomes according to the report. The recommendation is that carbon tax revenue should be raised by a carbon tax based on the heat content burnt as measured by the British Thermal Unit (BTU). However, this method favours dirtier fuels because coal, for example, produces far more pollution per unit of CO_2 than oil or natural gas. It is better to charge per tonne of carbon, which favours the cleaner fuels. Recommendations for carbon taxes around the world vary from $10 to $100 per tonne. The price of carbon will most likely depend on the severity of the climate crisis. 2015 greenhouse gas emissions in Australia were 549.3 Mt CO_2-equivalent according to the department of the environment.[15] At a rate of $10/ton the revenue would be total $5.49 billion and at $100/ton it would be $54.9 billion.

In previous discussions of carbon taxes with policymakers in Vermont, the figure of $100/ton evokes a somewhat shocked response that this is an inordinately high figure. To put it in perspective, consider that $100 per ton of carbon on a molecular weight basis is equivalent to almost $1 per US gallon of petrol (89c). According to the OECD the average petrol tax among the 34 advanced economies is $2.62 per gallon, and goes as high as $4.32 in Turkey.[16] So that is equivalent to a carbon tax of $294–485 per ton. From that perspective $100/ton of carbon is rather modest.

Summary

For the final calculation we start with total economic rent plus government revenue from monopolies of $386.9 billion. From this figure we subtract existing government revenue in each category so as not to shortchange government. To this we add new carbon tax revenue of $54.9 billion, leaving a total of $289.3 billion economic rent. Now that we have subtracted existing revenue, we can look at the total economic rent available for BI in Australia. Dividing the total of *$289.3 billion* by the current population of *24.05* million, results in a per capita BI of *$12,027*. This is an amount that others have arrived at from very different premises based on a subsistence level income. Some analysts are concerned that the work incentive will be reduced if the BIG is too high, and this figure would probably reassure them, since it is by no means exorbitant. If several members of a family were able to obtain this income, it might be enough to live on, but only barely enough unless the cost of housing was substantially reduced. It is based entirely on dividends that people are entitled to as their share of common wealth, and these figures demonstrate that it is also practical and feasible (Table 4.2).

Table 4.2 Economic rent minus existing revenue

Item	Valuation $million	% of valuation	Raised $million	Existing revenue $million	Remainder $million
Economic rent- land and resources				~2.5%	
Land – residential	2,794,800	5.50%	153,714	69,870	83,844
Land – commercial	338,500	6.5	22,002	8,463	13,540
Land – rural	263,700	5.50%	14,504	6,593	7,912
Land – other	287,700	5.50%	15,791	7,193	8,599
Total land	3,684,700		206,011	92,118	113,894
Subsoil minerals	67,359 +14.637	40%	32,813	–	–
Oil and gas – PRRT	20,229	40%	8,092	–	–
Total minerals and petroleum			40,905	1,500	39,405
Natural monopolies					
EMS	10,560	20%	2,122	1960/ 15=133.1	1,989
Corporate commons fee	1,382,000	2%	27,640	0	27,640
Water rights	50,000	2.60%	1,300	?	1,300
Utilities	220,000	10%	22,000	3,200	18,800
Airports	1,919	40%	765	0	765
Taxi licenses	25,000	14,402	360	7.4	352.6

Table 4.2 (continued)

Item	Valuation $million	% of valuation	Raised $million	Existing revenue $million	Remainder $million
Fishing licenses	2,100	40%	840	13.8	826.2
Forestry	1800	2.7%	50	1.3	48.7
Gambling license	18,450	40%	7,380	5,100	2,280
Public transport	estimate		2,400	74	2,326
Frontiers of monopoly					
Domain name registration	100	3 million	300	0	300
Patents	12,980	0.005%	65	0	65
Satellite orbit rights	5,100	10%	510	0	510
Internet infrastructure	64,500	10%	6,450	0	6,450
Banking license fees	43,427	40%	17,371	0	17,371
Existing revenues					
Parking fees	Estimate		250		0
Liquor licenses	Govt budget		4,000		0
Vehicle rego, driver license	Govt budget		5,294		0
Sin taxes - tobacco, alcohol	Govt budget		12,510		0
Carbon tax	4,020 +14,200		18,220	(18,220 repealed)	54,930
Govt non-tax receipts	20,323	50%	10,162		0
Total ($million)			$386,905		$289,252
Population (million)					24.05
BI per capita					$12,027

Notes

1. Chris Smith, "Bank of England: 95 million jobs going to robots in the next 10 to 20 years", November 16, 2015 http://bgr.com/2015/11/16/robots-replacing-human-jobs/.
2. Alaska Permanent Fund Corporation website: http://apfc.org/home/Content/home/index.cfm.
3. Adapted from Cambridge Energy Research Associates (CERA-defunct) "Ratcheting Down: Oil and the Global Credit Crisis", 2008.

4. Tomales Bay Institute, "State of the Commons Report": 2, 35, 2002–2003 http://bollier.org/commons-resources/commons-reports.
5. Dan Moss, The New Daily, "Cabinet Colleagues Jump to Hockey's Defence", June 10, 2015.
6. Alberta Department of Energy, "Let's Talk Royalties: Let's Talk About Norway", 2015 https://letstalkroyalties.ca/did-you-know/lets-talk-about-norway/.
7. Norwegian Ministry of Petroleum and Energy, "The Petroleum Tax System", (Update) November, 2016 http://www.norskpetroleum.no/en/economy/petroleum-tax/.
8. Robert O'Brien, The Eureka Report, "The Ultimate Liquid Asset", April 19, 2010 http://www.eurekareport.com.au/article/2010/4/19/commodities/ultimate-liquid-asset.
9. Stephen Dziedzic, ABC News, The World Today "Government Pushes States to Privatize Power", December 15, 2011 http://www.abc.net.au/news/2011-12-13/government-pushes-states-to-privatise-power/3727966.
10. Richard A. Oppel Jr., New York Times, "Word for Word/Energy Hogs; Enron Traders on Grandma Millie And Making Out Like Bandits", June 13, 2004 http://www.nytimes.com/2004/06/13/weekinreview/word-for-word-energy-hogs-enron-traders-grandma-millie-making-like-bandits.html?_r=0.
11. Clive Domain, Traveller, "The True Cost of Our Airports", August 29, 2011 http://www.theage.com.au/travel/blogs/travellers-check/the-true-cost-of-our-airports-20110829-1jha7.html.
12. "5310.0.55.002 – Information Paper: Implementation of New International Statistical standards in ABS national and International Account", Sept. 2009: http://www.abs.gov.au/ausstats/abs@.nsf/Products/5310.0.55.002~September+2009~Main+Features~Chapter+6%20Research+&+Development?OpenDocument.
13. Michael McLeay, Amar Radia and Rayland Thomas, Bank of England, "Money in the Modern Economy: an introduction", 2014Q1 http://www.bankofengland.co.uk/publications/Pages/quarterlybulletin/2014/qb14q1.aspx.
14. Michael Hudson, "America's Deceptive Fiscal 2012 Fiscal Cliff", Dec. 28, 2012 http://michael-hudson.com/2012/12/americas-deceptive-2012-fiscal-cliff/.
15. Department of the Environment, "Quarterly Update of Australia's National Greenhouse Gas Inventory": June 2015, http://environment.gov.au/climate-change/greenhouse-gas-measurement/publications/quarterly-update-australias-national-greenhouse-gas-inventory-june-2015.

16. Kyle Pomerleau, Tax Foundation, "How High Are Other Nations Gas Taxes?" March 3, 2015 http://taxfoundation.org/blog/how-high-are-other-nations-gas-taxes.

REFERENCES

Barnes, P. (2006) *Capitalism 3.0 A Guide to Reclaiming the Commons.* San Francisco: Berrett-Koehler.
Buxton, C. R. (2004) "Property in Outer Space: The Common Heritage of Mankind Principle Vs. The 'First In Time, First In Right' Rule of Property Law." *Journal of Air Law and Commerce* 69(4).
Fitzgerald, K. (2013) *Total Resource Rents of Australia, Harnessing the Power of Monopoly.* Melbourne: Prosper Australia.
Flomenhoft, G. (2016) *GST or Land and Resource Taxes? A Question Of Values.* (unpublished). Melbourne: Prosper Australia.
Locke, J. (1698) *Second Treatise of Government.* England: Awnsham Churchill.
Murray, C. A. (2008) "Guaranteed Income as a Replacement for the Welfare State." Basic Income Studies 3(2).
Paine, T. (1797), *Agrarian Justice: Opposed to Agrarian Law, and to Agrarian Monopoly,* London -eBook, Paris: printed by W. Adlard. London: re-printed for T. Williams, No. 8, Little Turnstile, Holborn.
Polanyi, K. (1944) *The Great Transformation.* Toronto: Farrar & Rinehart.
Snider, J.H. (2003) *The Citizen's Guide to the Airwaves.* Washington, D.C: New America Foundation.
Van Parijs, P. (1998) *Real Freedom for All, What if Anything Can Justify Capitalism?.* Oxford: Clarendon.
Warnock, J. W. (November 2006). *Oil and Gas Royalties, Corporate Profits, and the Disregarded Public.* Parkland Institute and Canadian Centre for Policy Alternatives – Saskatchewan Office
Widerquist, K., and M. Howard (Eds.) (2012a) *Alaska's Permanent Fund Dividend.* New York: Palgrave Macmillan.
Widerquist, K., and M. Howard (Eds.) (2012b) *Exporting the Alaska Model.* New York: Palgrave Macmillan.

Gary Flomenhoft is an International Postgraduate Research Scholar (IPRS) and University of Queensland Centennial Scholar and PhD candidate at the Centre for Social Responsibility in Mining (CSRM). His research area is the economic value of common wealth and governance of Sovereign Wealth Funds. Prior to enrolling at Sustainable Minerals Institute (SMI), Gary was a faculty member for 11 years in Community and International Development and Natural Resources at the

University of Vermont (UVM), serving as a Lecturer in Applied Economics, Renewable Energy, International Development, and Public Policy. He conducted many development projects in The Commonwealth of Dominica, St. Lucia, and Belize with students and local partners. He also originated and coordinated the Green Building Design Program at UVM. He had a secondary appointment as a Research Associate and Fellow at the Gund Institute for Ecological Economics under Director Robert Constanza. His primary research was in public finance for the state of Vermont including green/environmental taxes, common wealth and common assets, subsidy reform, and public banking. His 2013 report on Vermont public banking formed the basis of the "10% for Vermont" legislation passed in 2014, which allocated $35 million of state funds to local investment. He directed the grant-funded Green Tax and Common Assets project at the Gund Institute for seven years, where he originated the Vermont Common Assets Trust Fund (VCAT) bill, which was submitted to the legislature twice. His chapter on Vermont Common Assets appeared in the book Exporting the Alaska Model, which promotes the Alaska Permanent Fund and Dividend as a model for basic income around the world using Sovereign Wealth Funds.

CHAPTER 5

Conclusion

Richard Pereira

Abstract A review of the three basic income (BI) models and accompanying frameworks for creating a decent BI are presented in this chapter. A differentiation between positive and counterproductive BI proposals is made, particularly regarding the manner in which social services are treated in contrasting proposals. A wholesale approach to cutting public programmes is rejected as a financing model. Each chapter is then reviewed in this context, demonstrating how each achieves a progressive BI true to the definition of the concept.

Keywords Basic income models · Universal dividend · Demogrant · NIT (negative income tax) · Cost savings · Economic rent and taxation

The introductory chapter to this book presents three different BI models. The NIT (negative income tax), demogrant and a universal dividend are the three models discussed. The framework for understanding a *decent* BI and its financing is also described. A modest BI that is combined with elimination of most, or all, social programmes is not advocated in this book and is not viewed as a move forward. Universal public programmes

R. Pereira (✉)
University of Birmingham, Birmingham, UK

© The Author(s) 2017
R. Pereira (ed.), *Financing Basic Income*, Exploring the Basic Income Guarantee, DOI 10.1007/978-3-319-54268-3_5

such as health care in various countries are just one example of vital institutions that need to be maintained (and improved) to make the introduction of BI meaningful. Likewise, a low level of BI that preserves most public programmes can also be viewed as counterproductive. This book advocates a BI true to its definition, set at a sufficiently high level to cover basic needs and provide a measure of social inclusion, while preserving the most important public programmes.

It is recognized here that many bureaucratic programmes will naturally be eliminated, or reduced in size, with introduction of a BI, and that this is an entirely positive development. However, a wholesale approach to cutting public programmes is rejected as a financing method. Instead, it is argued that the cost savings available from programme redundancies has been greatly underestimated and even neglected in much of the BI literature – the costs have been overestimated without a comprehensive accounting of what programmes, tax deductions, tax shelters become redundant when people have guaranteed income security at a decent level.

The NIT model of BI demonstrates most clearly the cost savings available to governments by implementing a BI that can eliminate official poverty. Chapter 2 illustrates the large surplus that governments can achieve ensuring no one falls below the poverty line by way of a NIT BI. The cost of poverty is staggering and is often left out of BI costing assessments, as are related health care costs which are continually rising due to income insecurity and precarious employment.

Chapter 2 also explains how the "cost" (an actual savings of public funds) of the NIT version of BI is essentially equivalent to the demogrant version. The latter can be calibrated to produce the same results as the former. Demogrant versions of BI have what appears to be a larger upfront cost, often arrived at by making the very simple calculation of population (or adult population) × demogrant. What is often left out is that all currently employed persons will pay back all or most of their demogrant version of BI through existing personal income tax rates. These existing progressive personal income tax rates can be modified, or left as is.

Pereira demonstrates that the existing welfare system and the status quo of unnecessarily complex, bureaucratic income security programmes is too expensive (and oppressive). It also fails to achieve its purported objectives of universal income security. BI will be cheaper and fairer, and better achieve universal income security objectives. Not only does BI pay for itself given programme redundancies directly related to its implementation, but large-scale tax leakages and loopholes can simultaneously be

CONCLUSION 103

addressed to make for an even more robust BI along with improved complementary universal public programmes (health, education, legal aid, disability supports). The use of offshore tax havens is one major source of tax leakage discussed in the chapter.[1]

In Chapter 3 Jörimann details a BI plan for Switzerland at a decent level, which has relevance for other European jurisdictions with similar social programme infrastructure. This proposal includes CHF 2,500 per month for all adults and CHF 625 for minors. It is structured as a demogrant, and the NIT model of BI is not explored or compared for Switzerland. A gap of CHF 30 billion is arrived at between the cost of this demogrant proposal and the amount of funds which could be raised from the current system as a result of programme redundancies. Table 3.5 details a list of eight such programmes, which can be viewed as either fully or partially redundant with the implementation of BI and with these funds directed to its financing. It is a relatively short list of redundancies to consider, and items such as health care savings resulting from improved income security are also left aside (Dr. Evelyn Forget's work on the original BI experiments in Manitoba, Canada [Mincome] are relevant and worth consideration on this point).

Jörimann suggests as one possibility to complete the financing of his demogrant proposal "Redirecting funds from other sources... by taxing capital flows or gains" for example – sometimes referred to as unearned income. Financing approaches from other European thinkers are also put forth as options, such as Goetz Werner's value-added tax (VAT) proposal, other indirect taxes (including sin taxes and energy taxation, the latter intended to simultaneously address ecological imperatives while partially financing BI), or eliminating excessive tax exemptions for those who do not need them are all considered as options. Direct federal taxation of incomes is largely rejected as a method of partially financing a Swiss BI. "When it comes to a macro-economic view of the introduction of a fully-fledged BI, we state that the financing of the CHF 30 bn gap would not take funds from national consumer spending (which rather, is strengthened by BI because it tends to give more to those with less spending power); it would finance the gap from the savings pot."

Chapter 4 does not deal with programme redundancies as a model of financing BI. The question of economic rent is explained and explored for its potential to finance a universal BI, in the form of a universal dividend. "Windfall" profits that are gained from public resources, or commonwealth, ought to be distributed to the public that owns them. Successful

Sovereign Wealth Funds such as those in Norway and Alaska capture the value of one natural resource very well for the benefit of those societies, however, it is argued that there are many publicly owned natural resources from which wealth could be similarly captured for public benefit. Social resources also represent an important form of commonwealth as explained by Flomenhoft. If the windfall profits from these commonwealth resources were captured for a universal dividend the result would be a form of BI that could rival, or exceed, more traditional BI proposals at the highest levels. All without eliminating or scaling back any current government programmes or their associated bureaucracies.

The universal dividend model provides a large payment to all residents or citizens equally – children receive the exact same amount in annual payments as do adults. There is no age differentiation with this model of demogrant-dividend. Flomenhoft's proposal also addresses ecological imperatives by addressing carbon pricing by means of the fee and dividend model. Application of economic rent or windfall profit distribution is done conservatively throughout Flomenhoft's work, meaning that additional windfall profits are likely available to further boost the BI Guarantee (BIG) or universal dividend proposed.

Combining the concept of BI (in NIT or demogrant form) with a universal dividend based on rent as detailed by Flomenhoft could be the most transformative public policy proposal to address growing income insecurity. The first part entails largely addressing inefficient programmes, tax policies and bureaucracies to achieve a better system of income security. The second part (the universal dividend) focuses on windfall profits and actual public ownership of resources – or commonwealth – to distribute a dividend to all public owners of these common assets. "The democratic theory of rent simply says that people are entitled to these payments because it is their property. No one disputes that a person owning stocks is entitled to dividends, that an apartment owner is entitled to collection of rent from tenants, or an owner of an oil well is entitled to royalties," writes Flomenhoft.

It is also important to understand the illusion of progressive tax rate structures in many cases. While nominally progressive, once a myriad of tax loopholes, special exemptions and deductions, tax shelters and many other changes in the tax system over recent decades are factored in we often find tax regimes to be regressive as detailed in Pereira's work, or as early as in the Croll Report of 1971 which Pereira references. One part of this regressive structure is connected to how unearned income is often treated at much more favourable tax rates than earned income. In addition, "During this 'golden age for corporate profits' some of the largest multinational companies are paying zero tax, and receiving tax refunds and subsidies simultaneously," Pereira writes.[2]

FIVE KEY POLICY LESSONS FROM THIS STUDY

1. Personal income tax increases – taxes on labour or earned income – are not required to finance BI, which challenges a commonly used argument against universal BI. A personal income tax cut can be implemented along with introduction of a *decent* BI if so desired.
2. Public savings have been largely underestimated and many savings elements often neglected altogether in the BI literature, particularly in the cost objection literature. The list of naturally occurring redundancies of income security programmes, tax shelters and deductions arising from implementation of BI is much larger than usually discussed in the literature. Vital public and universal programmes such as health, education and others are not targeted for savings in this analysis; they are preserved and strengthened with introduction of a BI.
3. Tax leakage in various forms is significant and if addressed at *prevailing* taxation rates further strengthens the claim that no income tax increases are required to finance a BI, and that income tax rates could be cut while implementing a decent BI.
4. Economic rent must be considered in addition to traditional BI proposals. Whereas traditional proposals advocate the elimination of bureaucratic, oppressive, wasteful and often counterproductive income security programmes to be replaced by a superior payment in the form of a universal BI programme, the universal dividend based on rent can be paid to all individuals in addition to a decent BI. The dividend is an additional form of basic income following the demogrant model of delivery. It is financed by the capture of economic rent, or "windfall" profits, on various natural and social resources often termed common wealth. Alaska and Norway provide two examples of the capture of economic rent through their sovereign wealth funds, although narrowly based on one natural resource.
5. The cost objection to BI is based upon inadequate and/or misleading information. A comprehensive analysis of the costs and bureaucratic waste within the existing income security system will yield a different

conclusion than that found in the objection. Financing BI can produce fairer results for individuals and society while producing significant public cost savings. This can be seen perhaps most clearly in the costing of NIT models of BI yielding significant public savings while paying a high level of BI, which do not vary significantly from demogrant models of BI which can be calibrated to achieve the same results.

NOTES

1. The recent release of the Panama Papers is not addressed. The work of the International Consortium of Investigative Journalists (ICIJ) and the need for greater whistle-blower protections to further uncover such large-scale tax evasion and fraud can be found at: https://panamapapers.icij.org/. Tax Justice Network also has additional and continually updating news: http://www.taxjustice.net/topics/more/size-of-the-problem/ ("Size of the Problems").
2. Paul Buchheit, "16 Giant Corporations That Have Basically Stopped Paying Taxes – While Also Cutting Jobs!" *AlterNet*, 18 March, 2013.

Richard Pereira is Doctoral Researcher at the University of Birmingham, UK, and was formerly an economist with the House of Commons in Canada.

Appendix 1

Switzerland's Basic Income Referendum Results

The Swiss voted on five nationwide issues on June 5, 2016. One of these issues was the introduction of an unconditional basic income. 23.1% of votes were in favour (568,905), with 76.9% against (1,896,963). Several cantons voted about 35% in favour of basic income (Geneva 34.7% in favour, Basel 36%, Jura 35.8%).[1]

As SWI reported, "a few districts in the cities of Geneva and Zurich were in favour" with over 50% support in Geneva's Pâquis district for instance.[2] Although the overall result was clearly against the introduction of basic income at this time in Switzerland, those who organized the initiative which collected over 125,000 signatures within 18 months view the result as a success given how transformative the proposal is, and given the high level of basic income that was discussed nationally as a central feature of the initiative. A monthly basic income of 2,500 Swiss francs (£1,755; $2,555)[3] for adults and CHF 625 for each child had been suggested.

---

[1] SWI swissinfo.ch, "Vote results: June 5, 2016", 5 June, 2016.
[2] SWI swissinfo.ch, "The district that voted in favour of a basic income", 7 June, 2016.
[3] BBC News, "Switzerland's voters reject basic income plan", 5 June, 2015.

© The Author(s) 2017
R. Pereira (ed.), *Financing Basic Income*, Exploring the Basic Income Guarantee, DOI 10.1007/978-3-319-54268-3

Other measures indicate that this is the beginning of the debate, rather than the end. 69% of all voters believe they will be voting on another basic income referendum in the future.[4] Demographics, the rise of precarious labour, continued automation of jobs and other factors influence the changing political landscape and context in which public discussions of basic income will ensue. A refined discussion of the public financing options is necessary to provide the public with a clearer understanding of the cost and savings involved with such a proposal.

Two months following the Swiss referendum a detailed Canadian poll found the majority of Canadians supportive of a basic income, although 59% believed it would be too expensive to implement nationwide.[5] The same poll found 34% of Canadians would be willing to pay more in taxes to support a basic income. Therefore there is strong support for the concept, however there is a belief about the public cost of basic income that may not be supported by evidence and which may stem from popular perceptions or current political discourse. Interestingly, Canadians supported higher levels of basic income than lower levels, that is, $10,000 per adult (57% support), $20,000 (65% support) and a $30,000 annual basic income received 67% support.[6]

---

[4] Scott Santens, "The Results of the Basic Income Referendum in Switzerland", *medium.com*, 5 June, 2016.

[5] Angus Reid Institute (ARI), "Basic Income? Basically unaffordable, say most Canadians", 11 August, 2016.

[6] Angus Reid Institute, "Basic Income? Basically unaffordable, say most Canadians", 11 August, 2016. See section "Stronger support for higher basic income thresholds". Also, ARI found "Most Canadians (63%) believe...that new technology will reduce the availability of jobs, rather than increase it".

APPENDIX 2

MARGINAL PERSONAL INCOME TAX RATES: AMERICAN PRECEDENTS, VEILS OF IGNORANCE

The UBI cost objection does not deal sufficiently with tax leakage (tax havens, transfer pricing, etc.) in the existing system at prevailing income tax rates, as discussed earlier in this book. The cost objection argument states that income tax increases on labour are required to fund basic income, and that they would be too onerous and politically unacceptable. Yet historical precedent does exist for higher personal (and corporate) income tax rates, including at over 90% for the top income bracket in the US in the 1950s – under a Republican political administration. People did tolerate much higher marginal income tax rates and a much more progressive tax rate structure than the cost objectors claim is required in their analysis. Such high marginal tax rates were synonymous with a prosperous economy. And this among possibly the most tax-averse public in the world.

Employing John Rawls' concept of a "veil of ignorance" Dan Ariely (Professor of Psychology and Behavioural Economics, Duke University) and Mike Norton surveyed Americans in a unique study and found an overwhelming preference among both Democrat and Republican supporters for the wealth distribution profile in Sweden (93.5% of Democrats and 90.2% of Republicans) with no appreciable difference based on gender and income level of those surveyed. Moreover, the authors state "We found that the ideal distribution described by this representative sample of Americans was dramatically more equal than exists anywhere in the world" (Ariely 2012). Basic income cost objectors overstate their claims on not only the costs of UBI, but also in their linking of what is politically 'feasible' based on loose assumptions of what the public wants or will accept.

Even with all the misrepresentation and often excited claims against the financial cost of universal basic income, a larger percentage of Canadians support the concept of a guaranteed annual income than oppose it (Rainer and Ernst 2014; Trudeau Foundation 2013).[7] This book has demonstrated that increased taxes on labour are not required to fund a decent UBI. A personal income tax cut could even be realized while implementing basic income it has been argued, given the large-scale public savings available that have often been neglected in basic income literature. However, the context needs to be further clarified in terms of historical precedent and false claims about political feasibility put forth about what Canadians (or Americans) will accept in this regard.

Marginal Income Tax Rate
for the highest income bracket – US

Figures represent the rates in place at the beginning and ending year of each presidency.

Dwight D. Eisenhower

Marginal Tax Rate on **Regular Income over $400,000: 92% – 91%**
Maximum Tax Rate on **Long-Term Capital Gains: 25%**

John F. Kennedy

Marginal Tax Rate on **Regular Income over $400,000: 91%**
Maximum Tax Rate on **Long-Term Capital Gains: 25%**

Lyndon B. Johnson

Marginal Tax Rate on **Regular Income: Over $400,000: 91% – Over $200,000: 75.25%**
Maximum Tax Rate on **Long-Term Capital Gains: 25% – 26.9%**

---

[7] Also see Angus Reid Institute findings, August 2016, which can be found in Appendix 1.

RICHARD M. NIXON

Marginal Tax Rate on **Regular Income over $200,000: 77% – 70%**
Maximum Tax Rate on **Long-Term Capital Gains: 27.5% – 36.5%**

GERALD R. FORD

Marginal Tax Rate on **Regular Income over 200,000: 70%**
Maximum Tax Rate on **Long-Term Capital Gains: 36.5% – 39.875%**

JIMMY CARTER

Marginal Tax Rate on **Regular Income over $203,200 – $215,400: 70%**
Maximum Tax Rate on **Long-Term Capital Gains: 39.875% – 28%**
. . .

BARACK OBAMA

Marginal Tax Rate on **Regular Income: over $372,950 – over 388,350: 35%**
Maximum Tax Rate on **Long-Term Capital Gains: 15%**

Source: Fowler, M. (2012) "From Eisenhower to Obama: What the Wealthiest Americans Pay in Taxes," *ABC News*, 18 January [online].

Index

A
Alaska, 3, 5, 78, 82, 83, 104, 105n4
Alaska Permanent Fund Dividend, Permanent Fund Corporation, 78

B
Basic Income (BI)
  demogrant, 3, 5, 20, 101, 102, 103, 104, 105n4, 106
  NIT, 3, 20, 35, 101, 102, 103, 106
  Universal Basic Income(UBI), 10, 11, 12, 14, 16, 20, 25, 30, 31, 35
Bureaucracy, 10, 15, 28, 30, 31, 33, 35, 40n19, 41n25, 81

C
Canada Revenue Agency (CRA), Offshore Tax Informant Program, 26
Care work, 21
CERN (Conseil Européen pour la Recherche Nucléaire), 94
Charitable sector
  philanthropic giving and charity law, 39n12
  tax deductions, 17
  tax shelter schemes, 17

Corporate welfare, 4, 33, 34
Croll Commission, Report (1971), 22

D
DARPA (Defense Advanced Research Projects Agency), 93
Daycare, childcare, 21, 22
  night daycare, 21, 39–40n14
  overnight care, 21, 39n14
Democratic theory of rent, 79, 82, 104
  economic rent, 79, 82
Demogrant, 3, 5, 20, 24, 25–28, 31, 34, 35, 41n23, 101–104, 105n4

E
Earned income, 39n10, 58, 59, 62, 65, 66, 69, 70, 72, 73n11, 105
  See also Unearned
Economic multiplier effect, 13
Economic rent, 3, 5, 77–83, 85, 88, 89, 90, 91, 103, 104, 105n4
EITC (Earned Income Tax Credit), 24
  See also WITB [Canada]
Electromagnetic Spectrum, 83
EU, 94
Externalities, 10, 15, 31, 32, 34, 35, 37

F
Fee and dividend, 4, 34, 104
Food banks, 28
Forget, Evelyn, 103
France, 50–52
Free-riding, 10, 15, 31–34, 35

G
GDP, 12, 20, 21, 51, 52, 68, 91, 93
Germany, 50, 51, 52, 59, 60
GFC (Global Financial Crisis), 72, 78

H
Healthcare, 2, 19, 23, 24, 41n25, 51, 57, 102, 103

I
Individual Savings Account program (UK), 19
Internal Revenue Service (IRS), 111n8
International Telecommunication Union (ITU), 92, 93

J
Japan, 78, 94

K
Keynes, Maynard John, 78

L
Labour (forms of free labour being extracted), 32
Labour income, 10, 25, 32
Labour-market, 2, 13, 20, 31, 33, 34, 65, 67, 71
Labour standards, 40

Land rent, 79, 82, 84–85, 94
Liberal theory of rent, economic rent, 79, 82, 93
LICO (Low income cut-off), 12, 13, 38n6
Liquidity rent, 87
Locke, John, 79

M
Maternity, paternity leave, benefits, 20, 21
Mill, John Stuart, 78
Mincome, 103
Monopoly (rent), 89
Multiple jobholding, multiple job workers, 21
Murray, Charles, 2, 5n1, 81

N
Negative Income Tax (NIT), 3, 5, 20, 24–28, 31, 34, 35, 41n23, 41n28, 67, 102–104, 106
Norway, 5, 83, 85, 104, 105n4

O
Oil fund, 83

P
Paine, Thomas, 79
Pension(s)
  AHV – Switzerland, 53, 55, 58, 67, 71
  Canada Pension Plan (CPP)/Quebec Pension Plan (QPP), 16, 36
  Old Age Security (OAS) – Canada, 54–55, 73n11
Philanthropy, 83

INDEX 115

Precarious jobs, employment, precarity, 17, 22, 32, 102
Pregnancy, pregnant women and job dismissals, 21
Public trust resource, 88

R
Registered Retirement Savings Plan, 16
See also Tax shelters
Regressive taxation, 38–39n7
See also Taxes
Royalties, 78, 82, 104

S
Scarcity (rent), 89, 93
Social housing, 4, 20, 22, 23, 28, 40n21
Sovereign Wealth Funds, *see* Norway; Alaska; Oil fund
Speculation, 15, 32, 33, 60, 82
speculative activity, 64

T
Taxes
 carbon tax, 4, 95; carbon fee, 4; carbon levy, 4; fee and dividend, 4
 corporate taxes, 4, 85; cuts, 4; multinational companies, 27, 105; reductions, 4
 evasion, 4, 25, 26, 27
 personal income tax, 4–5, 10, 14, 15, 25–28, 32, 34, 102, 105n1
 regressive, 17, 38n7, 60, 104
 tax cuts, 4, 34, 35, 105; to corporate rates, 4; by implementing basic income, 4; neo-liberalism, 27, 52, 78
 tobin tax, 33(speculation tax[es])
 unearned *vs.* earned income, 17, 39n10, 82, 103, 104
 VAT, sales taxes, 38n4
Tax exemptions, 4, 60–61, 103
Tax-Free Savings Accounts (TFSA), 17, 19
See also Tax shelters
Tax havens, offshore tax havens, 26, 27, 103
Tax shelters, 4, 17, 39n12, 102, 104, 105n2
Transfer pricing, 26, 27

U
Underemployment, 17
Underground economy, 37n2
Unearned income (*vs.* earned income), 17, 18, 31, 39n10, 78, 82, 83, 103, 104
Unemployment, 53, 67, 81
United Kingdom (UK), 19, 27, 50, 88
United States (US), 4, 5n1, 22, 24, 34, 41n25, 78, 81, 87, 88, 93, 94, 95
Universal Basic Income (UBI), 3, 4, 9–28, 30–34, 38n4, 38n6, 39n10, 39n11, 40n19
See also Basic Income
Universal dividend, 3, 5, 101, 103, 104, 105n4
Universal public health care (or universal health care), 2, 23
Unjust dismissal, dismissal (pregnant women and employers), 21
Unpaid internships, 32
Unpaid overtime, 21, 32
Unpaid work, unpaid labour, 21, 32, 38n4

V
Van Parijs, Philippe, 11, 12, 25, 67, 82
Vermont (and public trust resources), 83, 88, 90, 95

W
Whistleblower protection, 106n1
White, Stuart, 11, 25

Windfall profits, 103, 104, 105n4
　See also Economic rent
WITB (Working Income Tax Benefit)
　See also EITC [US]
Workplace culture(s), 21
Workplace disability (and costs), 33
Workplace mental health, 33
Workplace standards violations, 40n17
　See also Labour standards

Printed in the United States
By Bookmasters